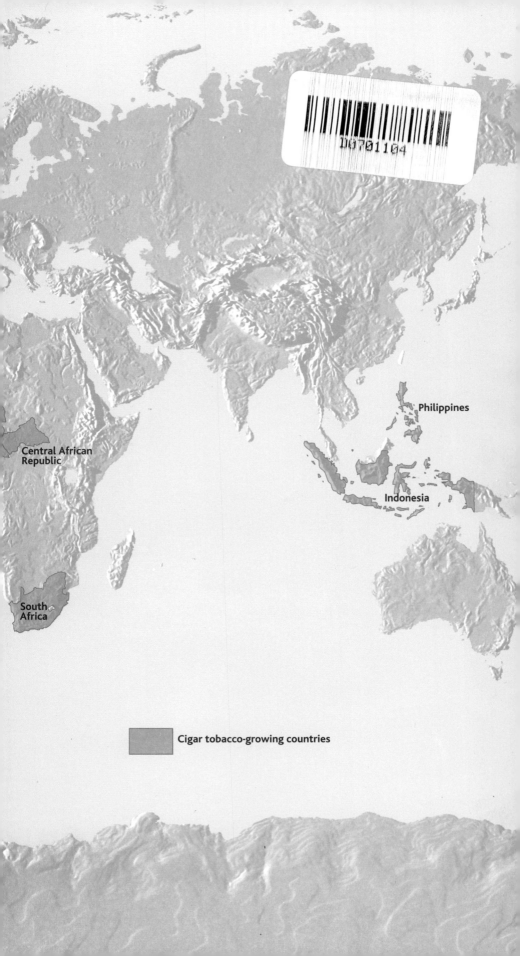

Philippines

Central African
Republic

Indonesia

South
Africa

Cigar tobacco-growing countries

THE COMPLETE GUIDE TO Cigars

THE COMPLETE GUIDE TO Cigars

STEVE LUCK

Bath · New York · Singapore · Hong Kong · Cologne · Delhi · Melbourne

First published by Parragon in 2008

Parragon
Queen Street House
4 Queen Street
Bath BA1 1HE, UK

ISBN: 978-1-4075-1603-5

Printed in China

CREATED AND PRODUCED BY **The Bridgewater
Book Company Ltd**
PHOTOGRAPHY **Paul Winch Furness, Ian Parsons**
MAPS **Mapping Ideas**
COVER IMAGES **Jeremy Horner/Corbis;
Image 100/Corbis**

Thanks to DAVIDOFFS (London) for their invaluable
assistance in the preparation of this book.

GOOD HEALTH

We all know that smoking is bad for our
health. The majority of cigar smokers don't
inhale – and nor should they. The pleasure of
savouring the flavour of a cigar that has been
created with care and attention should never
be confused with the desire for a nicotine
hit. If you feel you smoke too many cigars
try reducing the number you smoke, stop
altogether from time to time, or use nicotine
patches or gum.

CONTENTS

INTRODUCTION

There is no doubt that there is still something just a little bit glamorous about cigars. In this health-conscious age, this may seem somewhat surprising, although, possibly the long association between cigars and politicians, actors, comedians and musicians goes some way to explain this phenomenon. And, despite cigars being thought of as a male-only bastion, throughout much of cigar history a small group of women have also enjoyed lighting up a big cigar – and continue to do so to this day. There are a number of women-only cigar clubs and cigar dinners in both Europe and America, and in the latter in particular a number of high-profile women are happy to be photographed puffing on a premium cigar.

The cigar boom
The fascinating history of cigars begins in the eighteenth century, with the industry steadily increasing in popularity through the years, until the last fifteen years or so, when it experienced a major boom. Indeed, for much of the 1990s demand for premium, hand-rolled cigars in the United States and the Far East increased at a staggering rate, while European consumption enjoyed a distinct upturn. Hundreds of new brands appeared, along with numerous newly founded cigar bars and clubs. Even Havana, the premium cigar capital of the world, had trouble meeting demand.

Cigar Aficionado
A new lifestyle magazine *Cigar Aficionado* recorded and created much of the resurging interest. The magazine combined informative and well-researched articles on the world's major tobacco- and cigar-producing regions, their brands and the larger-than-life characters responsible for sustaining them, with reviews and comment on associated lifestyle products. It struck a nerve with people from all walks of life – and for a time, even the powerful and vociferous anti-smoking lobby couldn't dim the enthusiasm for this rekindled passion in hand-made cigars. But for the established aficionados the premium cigar world had started to sour. Their beloved old brands were often unavailable, replaced by more expensive and less agreeable cigars. In addition, some manufacturers were struggling to maintain decent

standards of quality control. By the end of the 1990s, the cigar party seemed to be over. Legislation prohibiting smoking in enclosed workspaces, including bars, pubs, restaurants and clubs, had come into force throughout much of the United States and Europe. However, surprisingly, the cigar industry appeared to be in good shape. Demand was down, for sure, but it was steady, and producers could concentrate on producing innovative and consistently well-made cigars.

The new world of cigars

With this in mind *The Complete Guide to Cigars* is designed as an invaluable source of reference for today's cigar world. Beginning with the history of tobacco, the book traces the development of the tobacco and cigar trade and its associated economic, political and cultural significance. An in-depth examination of cigars details how they are made, describes the recognized shapes and sizes, and explains how to select, store and smoke them. The book ends with an illustrated directory of famous cigar brands accompanied by actual-size examples, potted histories of each manufacturer and detailed information on individual cigars.

We hope that you will learn a little history, enjoy an anecdote or two, and gain an appreciation and understanding of an historical and supremely skilled craft.

1

THE HISTORY
OF CIGARS

THE ORIGINS OF TOBACCO

Perhaps the most poetic of the many myths surrounding the origin of tobacco derives from Huron mythology. This Native American tribe believed that the 'Great Spirit' sent a woman to provide for a starving world. Where she touched the soil, potatoes and corn grew; after a while she sat and rested, and when she stood, there grew tobacco.

◄ *This ancient Maya relief carving shows a figure smoking rolled-up leaves. The Maya word for smoking was* si'kar, *meaning 'to inhale smoke'.*

and experimented with tobacco from around 5000–4000 BCE; however, this again is speculation.

More concrete evidence becomes available, dating from around 1 BCE, which indicates that by this time the indigenous peoples of Central America regularly used tobacco for medicinal and ceremonial purposes, during which tobacco enemas were probably endured for the hallucinogenic visions they induced.

Maya civilization

The ancient civilization responsible for kick-starting the spread of tobacco use throughout much of the Americas was most likely the Maya. They were a once formidable and sophisticated people of the Yucatán Peninsula, Mexico, who mixed freely with other Meso-American civilizations and who, during what is referred to as the 'Classic' period (300–900 CE), established a branching network of trade routes that stretched south into South America and as far north as the Mississippi Valley of North America. The

Despite the myths, what is certain is that the tobacco plant first grew in the Americas; but exactly where no one can be sure. Some scientists believe it came from the Andes, others that its natural home was the region of modern-day Mexico. Nor can archaeologists be certain when the plant was first used by the indigenous populations of Central or South America, but it seems likely that they cultivated

first pictorial evidence of tobacco smoking can be dated from around this time – in the form of a pot on which is visible a Maya figure smoking rolled-up leaves tied together with string. In addition it has been suggested that the Maya word for smoking was *si'kar*.

Despite the gradual demise of Maya civilization from the eighth to the tenth century CE, its interaction with neighbouring peoples ensured that tobacco retained both its ceremonial and medicinal uses, albeit adapted to the specific customs and belief systems of the relevant tribes. For example, the Native American tribes of the Mississippi Valley region and beyond adopted tobacco smoking, mainly in the form of pipes, believing that their gods made themselves visible in the tobacco smoke.

After the Maya

Farther south in South America during the tenth to twelfth century CE, the Toltecs (probably ancestors of the Aztecs, who dominated Central America from the fourteenth to the sixteenth century) also inherited and adapted the custom of

▲ *This engraving by the sixteenth-century Flemish artist Theodore de Bry depicts Caraibes Indians smoking pipes during a ceremonial dance.*

tobacco smoking from the Maya. Evidence suggests that as well as smoking pipes, which tended to be the reserve of the ruling classes, those of lesser birth would also roughly roll together tobacco leaves to form a crude cigar, much as the Maya did before them.

Subsequently, the cult of tobacco would quickly have spread, eventually reaching the tribes of the Amazon Basin in modern Brazil and one group of Amerindian people in particular, the Arawak. Again evidence is scant, but we do know that it was the Arawak who settled on the archipelago chain of islands that today we call the Bahamas, and that it was descendants of the Arawak who would have greeted Columbus when he landed there in 1492.

◄ *Two men from the Yagua tribe from the Napo River in Peru smoke, dressed in their traditional grass skirts and headdresses.*

COLUMBUS, TOBACCO AND EUROPE

The sight of Columbus's ships must have made a resounding impression on the peoples of the Bahamas, the islands on which he landed on 12 October 1492. They presented him with extravagant gifts of 'fruit, wooden spears, and certain dried leaves which gave off a distinct fragrance', he wrote in his (now lost) journal.

◀ *This contemporary painting depicts Christopher Columbus being greeted by the indigenous people on his arrival in the Bahamas in 1492.*

World observed the local population smoking tobacco and ingesting a primitive form of snuff, and not long after they too had become confirmed smokers.

Tobacco in Europe

Traditionally, the first man credited with introducing the custom of smoking to Europe was Rodrigo de Jerez, who had accompanied Columbus on his first voyage to the New World. Jerez witnessed local tribes smoking when he explored Cuba, and on returning to his home town of Ayamonte in southern Spain was dispatched to prison by the Inquisition for spreading his 'sinful and infernal' habits.

This reference to dried tobacco leaves describes the first known European encounter with the plant. Although Columbus gratefully accepted the gifts – realizing the significance of the honour that the local tribe had bestowed upon him – he himself was less than impressed. The story goes that the fruit was eaten, the spears stored, but the unpleasant-smelling dried leaves cast away – and so their future impact on the world was lost.

However, it was not long before the true nature of the leaves was revealed. Sailors accompanying Columbus on his first and subsequent voyages to the New

The journals of the Spanish and Portuguese sailors, explorers and adventurers of the late fifteenth and early sixteenth centuries are littered with observations of tobacco smoking and chewing throughout the New World. Moreover, by the mid-sixteenth century the tobacco plant was increasingly perceived as a valuable and fashionable commodity, and one that boasted

numerous medicinal properties. In 1559 Philip II of Spain received a gift of tobacco seeds from his personal physician Francisco Hernández de Toledo. In 1560 Jean Nicot, the French ambassador to Portugal – and the man who gave his name to 'nicotine' – reported to the French court on the medicinal properties of the plant, and sent snuff to Catherine de Medici with word that it relieved migraine symptoms. A little later in England, Elizabeth I's favourite courtier, Sir Walter Raleigh, was responsible for spreading the fashion of smoking a pipe during the latter half of the 1580s.

Cash crop

By the end of the sixteenth century, tobacco, whether smoked through a pipe or taken as snuff or chewing tobacco, had gripped Europe. For many it was believed to offer comfort from sickness and disease, while for others it had become a symbol of status, wealth and fashion – but either way demand for tobacco grew at a phenomenal rate.

However, by the turn of the century the damaging effects of smoking were becoming increasingly apparent. In 1604 James I of England, in his treatise 'A Counterblaste to Tobacco', decried the habit of smoking. To combat the widespread use of tobacco James raised import tax by 4,000 per cent – from 2 pence per pound to 6 shillings 10 pence per pound. Unsurprisingly, revenue from tobacco imports in England fell drastically. The value of tobacco as a commodity, however, was quickly realized, and when James reduced import tax to 2 shillings per pound, the duty from tobacco came flooding in – and the financial incentive for establishing tobacco plantations was sown.

▶ A painting of King Philip II (c. 1570). The Spanish king became interested in the medicinal properties of tobacco, purely for commercial gain.

THE FIRST TOBACCO PLANTATIONS

Spanish and Portuguese sailors established tobacco farms in many regions of the New World during the late sixteenth century. By the early seventeenth century, the rising demand for tobacco in Europe saw more concerted efforts, particularly by Spain and England, to begin growing tobacco on an increasingly commercial scale.

Initially, Spain's southern, warmer territories in the New World of Central and South America were better suited to the growing of tobacco, and by the turn of the seventeenth century plantations were established in Venezuela, Puerto Rico, Cuba and other locations. Much of the crop was exported to England, with the revenue from its sale returning to Spain.

◄ The marriage of Pocahontas (c.1595–1617), the daughter of Powhatan, an important chief of the Algonquian Indians, to John Rolfe brought better relations between the settlers and Native Americans.

by local Native American tribes. Between 1609 and 1610 around 80 per cent of the population had died of disease, starvation or at the hands of the Native Americans. Although tobacco was grown near Jamestown, the flavour of the local variety, *Nicotiana rustica*, was too strong for the European market. John Rolfe, who had brought with him from Bermuda seeds of the more palatable variety, *Nicotiana tabacum*, established a good-sized plantation, and in 1612 the first commercial crop of tobacco was exported to England.

John Rolfe and Jamestown

In a deliberate effort to undercut the Spanish, a number of Englishmen attempted to establish tobacco plantations in the more northern English colonies of the New World. In 1609, following a voyage across the Atlantic that ended in his being shipwrecked in Bermuda, a merchant called John Rolfe eventually reached the struggling colonial town of Jamestown. Established by the Virginia Company of London two years earlier, Jamestown had suffered terrible hardships, including malaria and attacks

Within the space of a few years Rolfe had made his fortune. In the seventeen years from 1622 to 1639 the value of tobacco exports to England rose from £20,000 to a staggering £1.5 million; and by the end of the century the value had reached a colossal £20 million.

The slave trade

The social and economic impact of Rolfe's enterprise on the English colonies cannot be overestimated. Jamestown and other colonial settlements grew rapidly thanks to the revenue brought in by the tobacco plantations. Furthermore, these early plantations were the catalyst for the North American slave trade which changed the population dynamic in North America and the West Indies forever.

The first Africans were shipped to the plantations in 1619. Although these early African arrivals were not slaves, because they had been baptized and therefore as Christians could not be enslaved, the 'framework' for the trade was established, with the Virginia Assembly institutionalizing slavery in 1662.

The rapid and widespread growth of tobacco plantations in both English and Spanish colonies resulted in a massive increase in tobacco output, which not only made the trade harder to control financially but also led to a dramatic fall in quality. Both England under James I and Spain under Philip III introduced laws to protect the tobacco trade. In 1622 James I decreed that tobacco could not be grown in England, while in 1606 Philip ensured that all tobacco produced by the Spanish colonies was exported to one town in Spain, Seville, making that city the tobacco capital of Europe. Meanwhile in the English colonies, further tobacco plantations were established in Maryland and the Carolinas during the seventeenth and eighteenth centuries.

By the mid-seventeenth century, due to the scarcity of gold and silver, tobacco was being used as an alternative for currency in many Spanish and English colonial settlements. The practice of using tobacco as currency would continue for the next 200 years.

▼ *Africans were brought to the Americas as slaves to work on the tobacco plantations.*

TOBACCO HABITS

The majority of tobacco grown on New World plantations during the sixteenth and seventeenth centuries was used in rudimentary cigars in Spain, while in England pipes were preferred. The rapid rise in pipe smoking in England was demonstrated by the fact that even as early as 1614 tobacco was on sale in more than 7,000 outlets in London.

◄ *In the late seventeenth century laws were passed in Japan limiting the size of pipes because large, heavy pipes could be used as weapons.*

East, Japan and China tobacco use was banned altogether, often with hideous disfiguring punishments or a sentence of death placed on those who defied the law.

The age of snuff

In the seventeenth century the use of snuff became increasingly popular among the aristocracy in particular, especially in Spain and France. Perhaps they adopted snuff as a means of sidestepping local and national laws prohibiting the smoking of tobacco and because they perceived smoking to be so widespread as to be rife even among the lower classes. Charles II of England encountered the practice of snuff taking while exiled in Europe between 1647 and 1660, and it was he and his courtiers who were responsible for introducing snuff to England following the restoration of the monarchy in 1660.

However, the widespread smoking of tobacco was not without its opponents in Europe, such as James I of England (see page 13), and the rest of the world. During the mid- to late-seventeenth century many commentators and significant Church figures in England and elsewhere in Europe believed – somewhat ironically – that although smoking could be condoned on the grounds of warding off diseases and curing certain ailments, smoking for pleasure was immoral. While farther afield in Russia, parts of the Middle

For a while the taking of snuff remained an aristocratic pastime, but in 1702, so the story goes, when the English navy captured a number of Spanish ships many of the English sailors were paid in the snuff that was found aboard the Spanish vessels. The snuff was soon sold on to taverns and other stores in the ports and coastal towns of England, and in this way had reached the masses.

Snuff grew in popularity throughout the eighteenth century, and by the start of the nineteenth century it is thought that more tobacco was used in the manufacture of snuff than for use in pipes, cigars or for chewing. Among snuff's many advocates were Beau Brummel, Charles Darwin, Lord Nelson and Napoleon, who, it is alleged, used between one and two pounds of snuff every week.

Chewing tobacco

Meanwhile, the American colonies had also been enduring a love-hate relationship with tobacco smoking. While no one could deny that the growing of tobacco had almost single-handedly saved most of the fledgling settlements during the seventeenth and eighteenth centuries, an increasing number of laws were passed in various parts of America prohibiting or restricting the smoking of pipes. As a possible consequence, an increasing number of people turned to chewing

▲ Napoleon in his Apartments *by Jacques Onfroy de Breville. Napoleon was an avid snuff taker and had many beautiful snuff boxes in his possession.*

tobacco (instead of turning to snuff, as in Europe), but it is not easy to tell whether or not this was directly because of such legislation. Although the custom of chewing tobacco was as old as smoking and snuff taking, the colonists invented ways of flavouring the tobacco with a variety of products, including whisky and chocolate. By the turn of the century, in the American South at least, chewing tobacco was by far the most common way of taking the leaf. On the wider global stage, however, another product was beginning to assert itself – the cigar.

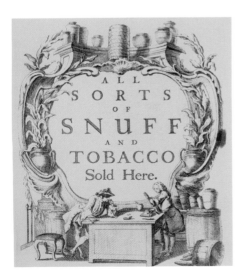

◀ *'All Sorts of Snuff and Tobacco Sold Here.' An eighteenth-century copper engraving advertising the sale of snuff and tobacco.*

THE FIRST 'SEGARS'

Although opinion differs slightly on when cigars were first produced in any great quantity, we do know that Seville, in Spain, is widely accepted as the birthplace of the modern cigar during the first half of the eighteenth century, and that its popularity spread from there to the rest of Europe over the course of the next 50 years.

Following Philip III of Spain's decree in 1606, enforcing all tobacco grown in the Spanish colonies to be shipped to Seville, the city became the European capital of Cuban tobacco, and it was here that the first cigar factories were established. There is little recorded evidence as to who was responsible for developing cigars, known as *Sevillas*, after the city in which they were made. Although we know that many ancient pre-colonial societies smoked tobacco leaves rolled up in maize husks or palm leaves, these were a far cry from the carefully hand-crafted cigars of modern times.

▲ *A depiction of the celebrations held to mark the end of the Seven Years' War in 1763. The cost of the war saw England enforce increasingly draconian tax laws on the colonies, eventually leading to the Revolutionary War, or War of Independence.*

Cigars and Britain

Although cigar factories were established north of Spain, notably in France and Germany, during the late eighteenth and early nineteenth centuries, cigars remained relatively unknown in England until the advent of the Peninsular War (1808–14). British servicemen readily took to smoking the Spanish *Sevillas* during this conflict in Spain, when British, Portuguese and Spanish forces formed a coalition to oust the invading French

◄ *The American army officer and farmer Israel Putnam (1718–90) brought back cigars and tobacco seeds from Havana to Connecticut.*

forces under Napoleon. The popularity of 'segars', as the British soldiers called them, spread rapidly upon their return to Britain, and it wasn't long before cigar factories were established in Britain, with some attempting to utilize the fledgling technology of the Industrial Revolution. The rapid growth of the industry resulted in an Act of Parliament (1821), the purpose of which was to regulate cigar production.

Cigars and America

The early history of the cigar in colonial North America is perhaps less easy to trace. One theory is that Israel Putnam, a future American general in the War of Independence, or Revolutionary War, was responsible for popularizing cigars in America. The story runs that in 1762 Putnam fought alongside the British during their capture of Havana as part of the complex global conflict known as the Seven

▲ During the Peninsular conflict in Spain (1808–14) British soldiers, fighting alongside the Spanish, began to smoke Spanish cigars known as Sevillas.

Years' War (1756–63). On his return to Connecticut, where he owned a tavern and a farm, Putnam brought with him some Cuban cigars and some tobacco seeds. The cigars he sold in the tavern and the seeds were used to start tobacco plantations in the Hartford area of Connecticut, so giving rise to the famous Connecticut Shade leaf, which is used as a wrapper today for some of the world's finest cigars.

Although there is evidence to support these claims, cigars did not immediately replace the pipe or chewing tobacco until much later. The story of the cigar in America still had a long journey to run, one involving revolution, a war in Mexico and a bloody civil war that was to cost the lives of more than 600,000 soldiers.

TOBACCO, REVOLUTION AND WAR

Tobacco plantation, cultivation and usage during the American War of Independence was a highly significant factor. For many of the tobacco-growing colonies, notably Virginia, the war was known as the 'Tobacco War'. Indeed, George Washington, leader of the American army and future first President of the United States, was himself a tobacco planter.

Put simply, the American War of Independence (1775–83) resulted in large part from the cost to the British of the Seven Years' War (1754 and 1756–63) some 20 years earlier, during which British and colonial forces successfully pushed France out of North America, defeated those Native Americans who had aligned themselves with France, and regained Florida from Spain (in return for Cuba).

▲ *A 1783 map of America showing the President, George Washington, on the left and one of the Founding Fathers of the United States, Benjamin Franklin, on the right.*

'No taxation without representation'

To pay for continued British military protection, the colonies, many of which felt that they had already paid their fair share for British military support, were forced to endure greater and greater taxation in various forms imposed by George III's British government. The economic impact resulted in massive debt among many of the colonial settlements, not least the tobacco growers, and this soon nurtured a desire for political independence among the 13 colonies – a burgeoning political will that was perhaps best described in the famous phrase, 'no taxation without representation'.

Tobacco certainly helped pay for the ensuing war against the British. For example, Benjamin Franklin secured a loan from France using five million pounds of Virginia tobacco as security, and, when the war was over, tobacco taxes certainly helped to repay much of the war debt.

The Mexican War and American Civil War

As we know, cigars were relatively unknown in North America up until the mid-nineteenth century, especially in the South where the vast majority of planters'

crops were used to make chewing tobacco. But with many American soldiers serving in Texas during the Mexican War (1846–48), where *cigarros* and *cigarillos* were much more common, cigars became increasingly widespread and their popularity grew.

By the time of the American Civil War (1861–65) cigars, particularly 'Havanas' (the name given to cigars made from Cuban tobacco), were increasingly perceived as a status symbol, although it was to be some years before cigars exceeded chewing tobacco in popularity, particularly in the South. One significant impact of the war was that this was the first time in which many Union soldiers from the North had come into contact with tobacco, in the form of rations.

By the end of the nineteenth century, cigars had become firmly entrenched in North American society. Cigar factories using both Cuban and domestically grown tobacco had sprung up in many regions of the country, but most notably in Florida, the home of Ybor City, Tampa (see pages 28–9).

CIGARS IN EUROPE

In Europe in the mid-nineteenth century cigars were already widely accepted in fashionable society. The popularity of cigars increased over the next 50 years, where certainly in England it was customary for ladies to withdraw to the drawing-room after dinner to allow the gentlemen to enjoy their cigars with an after-dinner port or brandy.

◄ *The increasing popularity of cigar smoking led to the creation of high-quality cigar accessories, such as this silver-plated cigar lighter.*

testament not only to the increased wealth of the growing middle classes but also to the status that a good cigar could bestow upon its owner.

Fashion and royalty

Smoking cigars even influenced the fashion of the day. At home with male friends, many English gentlemen would don 'smoking jackets' to enjoy a cigar in the evening. Often brightly coloured, the jackets were made of luxurious velvet or silk, cashmere or decoratively patterned flannel, and were usually accompanied

The vast amount of cigar-related Victoriana now for sale on internet auction sites is evidence of how firmly entrenched and fashionable the cigar had become in many countries across late nineteenth-century Europe. Exquisitely hand-painted, papier-mâché cigar cases, gold-plated table cigar lighters featuring family crests, and highly decorated brass, silver and gold cigar cutters are readily available, and most command very high prices. All are

► *Edward VII of England enjoying a cigar. It is said that the day after having an operation to remove his appendix, he enjoyed a recuperative cigar.*

with a fez-like, brimless cap that prevented the cigar smoke permeating the wearer's hair. Furthermore, in England the ranks of cigar devotees were swelled by the Prince of Wales, who apart from being the future king of England (as Edward VII) was also considered the epitome of fashion.

The Prince of Wales started the fashion for wearing a 'cut-down' version of the tailcoat, formally worn during dinner. An American businessman, James Brown Potter, when invited to one of the formal dinners attended by the Prince of Wales, had a similar semi-formal dinner jacket made on the advice of the Prince. The dinner jacket, much more comfortable than the long tailcoat, became the rage in England. On his return to New York, Potter, who lived in an upmarket district known as Tuxedo Park, introduced the dinner jacket to his circle, and for a few months the Tuxedo 'set' raised eyebrows in the various

▲ By the nineteenth century smokers' clubs were popular in England. Men would gather in such places to socialize, drink and smoke. Cigar smoking was by now firmly entrenched in fashionable society.

upmarket eating establishments with their daring new attire – and so the tuxedo was born (which incidentally the French still call 'le smoking').

Across Europe, the introduction of smoking carriages on trains, and smoking rooms in clubs and hotels, was further evidence of the popularity of cigars. Cigars from Cuba were considered the finest of them all. The popularity of Cuban cigars can probably be traced back to Ferdinand VII of Spain, who during the 1820s and 1830s encouraged the production and importation of Cuban cigars; being a Spanish state monopoly, their sale generated a great deal of money for Spain. And so the story of cigars now shifts back to the Caribbean.

CUBA AND TOBACCO

Tobacco was first cultivated in Cuba during the second half of the sixteenth century, by which time the island had become an established Spanish colony. During the next three centuries, the rapidly growing European market for tobacco saw tobacco plantations literally grow up all over the island.

◄ *An artist's impression of a Cuban tobacco plantation in the late nineteenth century. By this time, cigars were exported in their millions.*

The earliest tobacco plantations in Cuba were located on the banks of the Almendares River, which feeds into Havana. It is estimated that by 1602 the population of Cuba was about 20,000, of which some 14,000 lived in or around Havana and farmed. While sugar cane was their main product, tobacco was always a significant crop in terms of revenue.

The long arm of Spain

The importance of controlling the tobacco industry was recognized by Spain, which throughout the seventeenth and eighteenth centuries passed numerous laws restricting tobacco cultivation and its sale, ensuring that tobacco production was kept in check, that smuggling was severely dealt with and that the Crown was the beneficiary of all tobacco-generated revenue. In 1603, for example,

Spain decreed that the sale of tobacco to a non-Spaniard was punishable by death, while in 1614, although certain restrictions on the cultivation of tobacco were lifted, all tobacco had to be exported to Seville, southern Spain, where in 1620 the world's first tobacco-processing plant was built. At this time most of the tobacco growers were expatriates from the Canary Islands and other regions of Spain, who were encouraged by the Spanish government to settle in Cuba to take on the responsibility of fostering this new important cash crop.

Estanco de Tobacco

The continued and often harsh interference from Spain, culminating in the establishment of the *Estanco de Tobacco* (or *Factoria*) in 1715 – a measure that created an official monopolizing body responsible for purchasing all Cuba's tobacco at a set price – resulted in the uprising of the tobacco growers, or *vegueros*. Further revolts occurred in 1720 and 1723. The uprisings were sufficiently well supported to force the island's governor to flee to Spain. The insurrection, however,

▲ The Partagás factory in Havana, Cuba, established in 1845. By 1900, the factory was making 18–20 million cigars a year.

was short-lived and following the arrival of new troops from Spain, the ringleaders were rounded up and executed. However, the strength of feeling among the tobacco growers and other Spanish settlers, combined with the ever-shifting balance of power in Europe and Cuba's financially significant relationship with the United States, resulted in a gradual move by the Spanish government towards more relaxed trading restrictions.

From tobacco to cigars

It's important to remember that up until the beginning of the nineteenth century, although there was some small-scale cigar production in Cuba, the majority of cigars smoked in Europe were manufactured in European factories using Cuban tobacco. But this situation was about to change.

In 1817, Spain renounced the *Estanco* with the *Decreto Real*, allowing foreign privately owned companies to produce and sell Cuban cigars and tobacco. Combined with the increasing popularity of the superior Cuban-made cigars in Europe, this measure heralded the start of massive economic growth on the island. In 1827 cigar exports grew to almost half a million, but by 1836 that figure had risen to five million. Shortly thereafter, some of the most enduring Cuban cigar brands were established, including Punch (1840), Partagás (1845) and H. Upmann (1844).

▶ An engraving of the port at Havana during the 1720 uprising, when tobacco growers forced to sell at a set price revolted against the island's governor.

CUBAN CIGARS AND INDEPENDENCE

By 1827, 5,500 tobacco plantations existed in Cuba and this figure was to rise to 9,500 by 1859. Cigar factories also sprang up all over the island, with as many as 1,300 operating by the middle of the nineteenth century. The cigar had become Cuba's national symbol and cigar makers made up the vast majority of the Cuban industrial class.

◀ *United States volunteers gather in 1851 in one of the many Florida camps, as part of a popular movement to wrest Cuba from the Spanish.*

It's difficult to fully assess the role of cigar workers in Cuba's fight for independence, which was finally achieved in 1902. But as already noted, they made up the majority of the industrial workforce, and thanks to the longstanding tradition of the *lector*, or reader, most cigar workers were surprisingly well informed. The idea of the *lector* began at the El Figaro cigar factory, which was established in Havana during the 1860s. The role of the *lector* was to keep the 300 or so cigar workers entertained. He would read out loud the novels by famous writers of the day, together with articles from newspapers and pamphlets. Moreover, with the struggle for independence growing as the turn of the century approached, it was only natural that the *lector*'s readings became increasingly politicized so that the workers could be updated on the struggle.

Despite America's official neutral stance on the question of Cuban independence, there were powerful voices in the southern

states that supported annexation of Cuba, and they were joined in Cuba by the wealthy plantation and factory owners, and the workers themselves. The growing civil unrest in Cuba between the pro-independence forces and Spanish forces and their supporters in Cuba (later to become known as Cuba's Ten Years' War), combined with high American tariffs, which forced up the price of Cuban cigars, resulted in a large number of cigar manufacturers moving their operations to the United States (see pages 28–9), and to Kingston, Jamaica. Many self-exiled Cuban cigar producers were responsible for funding the continuing struggle against Spanish rule. José Martí, one of the key figures in Cuba's fight for independence and a present-day national hero, is alleged to have sent orders for the start of a major insurrection from Key West to Cuba inside a cigar – a poignant and symbolic act.

▲ *Cuban fighters in the 1895 War of Independence. Cuban soldiers, known as* Mambises, *were outnumbered five to one by the Spanish.*

The Spanish-American War

Cuba's fight for independence, which resulted in an increasingly unstable country, caused grave concern in the United States. In response to America's threat of war, Spain then declared war on America in April 1898. The ensuing Spanish-American War only lasted from April to August of that year, but it resulted

in the end of Spanish rule in the whole of the Caribbean; and by 1902 Cuba was an independent nation, albeit an unstable one that was faced with huge social and financial difficulties due to centuries of Spanish mismanagement.

With Spain's defeat, American-owned companies (mostly run by the established Cuban cigar families) began to dominate the Cuban cigar industry, which underwent a period of massive restructuring. This resulted in a reduction in the number of factories from over 1,000 in the 1850s to around 120 by 1900.

▼ *US soldiers arriving in Cuba in 1898, the final year of the War of Independence. The next conflict, the Spanish-American War, ended Spanish rule.*

YBOR CITY AND THE CUBAN INVASION

The massive social unrest in Cuba during the fight for independence, combined with high American tariffs on Cuban cigars, resulted in many Cuban cigar makers moving their factories to Florida, primarily in areas around Key West and Tampa. One such factory owner, Vicente M. Ybor, was to forge the way.

Vicente Martinez Ybor was born in Valencia, Spain, in 1820. When he was 14, his parents moved to Cuba, where the young Vincente became increasingly interested in cigar manufacturing. After gaining knowledge of the cigar industry as a cigar salesman, Ybor decided to set up his own factory in Havana in 1853. As the civil unrest in Cuba grew in intensity, Ybor decided that the future of his cigar business lay in the United States.

▼ *Port Tampa in Florida, 1904. After the social unrest created by the Cuban War of Independence, many cigar manufacturers relocated to Key West and Tampa in Florida.*

From Key West to Tampa, Florida

In 1869 Ybor decided to move his entire factory, and workers, to Key West, Florida. Although his factory became well established and relatively successful, the lack of a local labour force, a fresh water supply and a poor transportation infrastructure held back growth, and Ybor began to look for other areas in which to expand his business.

A fellow Spaniard, Gavino Gutierrez, who was familiar with Florida through his citrus fruit business, persuaded Ybor, along with another factory owner, Ignacio Hoya, to visit a small town called Tampa as a potential site for cigar factories. Tampa had recently joined the main railroad link, and the businessman, Henry B. Plant, responsible for bringing the railroad to Tampa was also setting about improving the town's port facilities. These newly installed transportation

links, through which Ybor could import all the tobacco he needed from Cuba and then distribute his cigars to the American north, combined with a humid climate appropriate for cigar manufacturing and a good freshwater supply, impressed Ybor. In 1885 he bought 40 acres of land on the outskirts of the town, where he began work on a new factory. In 1886 Ybor's factory in Key West burned down, and he moved his entire operation to Tampa.

▲ *The cigar factory at Ybor City in Tampa, Florida. The extensive Ybor factory became a town in the 1890s, and thrived until the Great Depression of 1929.*

The cigar capital of the world

Ybor's factory in Tampa and the accommodation he built for his workers and their families grew rapidly, and in the period between 1880 and 1890 the population of Tampa and the newly incorporated Ybor City grew from 800 to over 5,000. Ybor City expanded to become a thriving, bustling multiethnic town, its immigrants coming from Cuba, Spain and other European countries. By 1900 Ybor City was producing more hand-made Cuban-tobacco cigars than Havana. Throughout the 1920s Ybor City continued to grow, but the Great Depression of 1929 and the growing popularity of cheap mass-produced cigarettes resulted in a decline in the Cuban cigar market. Throughout the 1940s and 1950s much of the population of Ybor City moved away to find work elsewhere, and in the mid-1960s a section of the old city was demolished to make way for an interstate in the United States.

◀ *Ybor City Museum celebrates its heritage in 1999. In its heyday the area produced over 250 million cigars a year, and for over half a century was thought of as 'the Cigar Capital of the World'.*

BOXES AND BANDS

As the Cuban cigar industry grew and was reorganized throughout the nineteenth century, identifiable brands began to emerge. The history of most key brands is covered in the Cigar Directory section, but here we'll look at the evolution of the generic box of Cuban cigars and their bands, which involved extremely high-quality lithographic printing.

◄ *A Cuban factory worker assembling a cigar box, c. 1910. Before the arrival of the cigar box, cigars were sold in bundles covered with pigs' bladders.*

The exact details of the emergence of the first cigar box are unclear, but the idea is generally credited to the H. Upmann brand of cigars. Legend has it that two German brothers, having set up a bank in Havana, used small cedar boxes containing 25 cigars and stamped with the name H. Upmann as promotional gifts to their favoured customers. The cigars and their boxes were so popular that the Upmann brothers decided to establish their own factory and cigar brand in 1844.

Box art

The stone lithographic printing process first arrived in Cuba around 1827, with the establishment of the Havana Lithographic Workshop. The first brand of cigars to exploit this printing process to decorate its boxes is generally thought to be Ramón Allones, a brand that was established in 1845 by two Spanish brothers, Ramón and Antonio. As well as playing their part in decoration and marketing, the illustrated boxes were also stamped with a registration mark, a process that all cigar manufacturers were legally obliged to undergo. As the lithographic process

Before the emergence of recognizable brands of cigars and before the large factories were established, cigar brokers in Havana would simply pay tobacco farmers for the cigars they rolled, collect the cigars and ship them to Europe in huge cedar chests containing between 5,000 and 10,000 cigars. Although on the whole the cigars were better made than those in Europe and contained the much sought-after Cuban tobacco, their quality varied.

was refined and improved, the box designs became increasingly colourful and ornate, culminating in the addition of gold embossing around 1880. Today's cigar boxes, both Cuban and non-Cuban, feature all sorts of information stamps about the production method, the manufacturer, the year of the tobacco crop and more (see pages 72–3).

Cigar bands

Bands are thought to have been introduced by Gustave Bock, a Dutchman who became active in the Havana cigar industry during the 1830s. Bock's idea was that the band would differentiate his cigars from other brands, and would deter cigar vendors in Europe from selling non-Cuban cigars. The cigar band also prevented gentlemen from staining their white gloves when smoking a cigar.

▶ *A modern artwork on a Ramón Allones cigar box. Allones was the first manufacturer to decorate his cigar boxes in the 1840s.*

▲ *H. Upmann's cigar factory in Havana. Upmann is credited with the introduction of the cigar box and went on to establish his own factory in 1844.*

Most brands feature cigars that are available in aluminium tubes often wrapped in a very thin layer of cedar. These cigars will have 'tubos' as part of the name. Usually sharing the same vitola as another cigar in the same range, the tubed cigars are rounder, since boxed cigars can become slightly flattened in their boxes.

RAMON ALLONES

FLOR·EXTRA·FINA

HABANA

RAMON ALLONES

MADE IN HAVANA, CUBA

THE CUBAN REVOLUTION

When Fidel Castro overthrew General Fulgencio Batista in 1959, he implemented a whole raft of Marxist policies that saw the nationalization of both Cuban and foreign-owned companies, including the many American-owned cigar-manufacturing businesses, all of which were eventually put under the control of Cubatabaco, a state-owned monopoly.

Castro's appropriation of American-owned assets on the island angered President Dwight D. Eisenhower's administration. Relationships between the United States and Cuba soured further following the unsuccessful Bay of Pigs invasion in 1961, during which CIA-funded Cuban exiles attempted to overthrow Castro. In a bid to protect himself from further attack, Castro aligned himself with the USSR, which ultimately saw the Soviets attempt to erect nuclear missile bases on Cuba in 1962, an episode known as the Cuban Missile Crisis.

In response to Castro's alignment with the Soviet Union, the United States under President John F. Kennedy imposed an embargo on Cuba in 1962, making illegal the importing of any Cuban goods into America – however, not before Kennedy had acquired 1,200 H. Upmann Petit Coronas by way of his press secretary Pierre Salinger the night before the embargo was due to take effect. In fact, at one point in early 1962 it was hoped that Cuban cigars would be exempt from the embargo, but, according to Salinger, Kennedy revealed that the 'cigar manufacturers in Tampa objected. I guess we're out of luck.'

Post revolution

In many ways Cuba's cigar industry, despite being nationalized, suffered relatively little due to the US embargo during the subsequent 30 years. Although the number of brands dropped from 140 in 1959 to fewer than 40 in 1962, the number of individual cigars exported remained relatively constant. After an initial drop in exports between 1961 and 1963, the nationalized industry recovered and the rest of the world was able to (and

▶ *Fidel Castro enjoying a cigar. It is said that he smoked Cohíbas – considered to be one of the world's finest cigars.*

▲ Women waiting in line for food in 1964. Despite hardships caused by the United States embargo, the Cuban cigar industry has remained healthy.

still does) enjoy Cuba's premium cigars, the demand for which has generally outstripped production.

Arguably the most significant upshot of the US embargo was the desire by former Cuban cigar producers, such as the Palicio, Cifuentes and Menendez families, to establish factories outside Cuba. The result was that numerous former well-known Cuban cigar brands, most of which appear in the Cigar Directory, were re-established using the same or similar names elsewhere causing a certain amount of confusion on the international cigar markets.

'The Special Period in Peacetime'

Of much greater concern to the Cuban cigar producers was the dissolution of the Soviet Union in 1991. Throughout much of the latter half of the twentieth century, Cuba relied almost entirely on the Soviet Union for its export markets and for essential imports, most notably oil. Without the support of Comecon, Cuba entered what was referred to as the Special Period in Peacetime, during which major changes in agricultural practice, a drastic reduction in the use of cars and buses, a general move towards a more vegetarian diet and strict rationing enabled the Cuban people to avoid widespread hunger and ill-health.

Throughout the Special Period, however, the tobacco industry was again relatively unaffected, and although exports fell to around 50 million in 1993, the late 1990s witnessed a steady increase in exports, approaching 150 million in 1999. But such high production figures caused the quality of Cuban cigars to fall dramatically.

◀ President Kennedy with his press secretary Pierre Salinger in 1960. Salinger acquired Cuban cigars for the President the night before the embargo.

CUBA'S TOBACCO-GROWING REGIONS

Cuban cigars have been fêted throughout their history largely because Cuban tobacco is widely regarded as the finest in the world, although many of the other tobacco growers around the world would disagree on that point. But exactly what is it about this Caribbean island that lends itself so well to tobacco cultivation?

Although there are some tobacco-growing regions in the eastern and central regions of the island, by far the most significant area for tobacco cultivation is found at the western end of Cuba. This area is the location of Pinar del Río, the westernmost province and Cuba's third largest.

Covering almost 11,000 square kilometres (4,200 square miles), the province is home to around 750,000 people, most of whom are involved directly or indirectly in the cultivation of tobacco – the region producing around 70 per cent of Cuba's entire tobacco crop.

Vuelta Abajo

Pinar del Río province is also the home of one of Cuba's three main mountain ranges, the Cordillera de Guaniguanico, which is divided into the Sierra del Rosario to the east and the Sierra de los Órganos to the west. Between the mountains lie flat, fertile valleys featuring a rich red, sandy loam soil that is ideal for growing tobacco, and one region in particular, the Vuelta Abajo, is highly prized.

The Vuelta Abajo covers about 40 hectares/100,000 acres and is divided into small plantations, or *vegas*, most of which are between 2 and 4 hectares

▲ *Cuba's tobacco-growing regions, the most important of which are concentrated in the west of the country.*

Tobacco regions

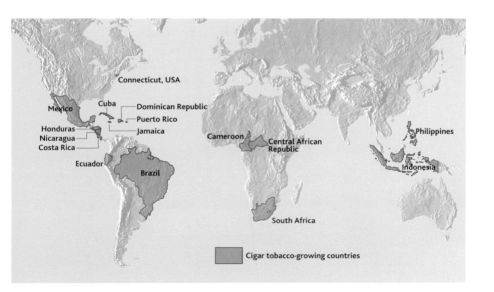

▲ *A map showing the world's main cigar 'tobacco-growing' regions. Only the highest-quality tobacco is used to produce premium cigars.*

(5 and 10 acres) in size, with some as large as 60 hecatares (150 acres) – the maximum amount of land a *veguero* (smallholder) can own. Within the Vuelta Abajo itself, lies one small area that is particularly renowned for its tobacco. Here around 1,000 hectares (2,500 acres) are cultivated specifically for the highest quality wrappers, and some 2,000 hectares (5,000 acres) for fillers and binders. This small region is where Cuba's most famous tobacco farmer, Alejandro Robaina, nurtures his crop.

Sun and rain

The high quality of the tobacco from Pinar del Río is due not only to the region's fertile soil and undulating landscape, the *terroir*, but also to its climate. During the growing season – October or November to February – the region gets on average eight hours of sunshine each day and humidity is high, which make for ideal conditions. It receives 170 cm (67 in) of rain each year on average, with only around 23 cm (9 in) falling during the growing season, again ideal.

Another important growing region in Pinar del Río is the Semi Vuelta, an area that produces stronger-tasting tobacco, which is generally used in the domestic market. Outside Pinar del Río there are tobacco plantations south-west of Havana. Known as the Partido, this region produces wrapper tobacco for use in premium cigars. The other regions, Remedios in the centre and Oriente in the far south-east of the island, produce tobacco for bulk export and for use in cigarettes respectively.

THE DOMINICAN REPUBLIC

When the US embargo of Cuban products was established in 1962, Cuba lost its most significant cigar market overnight; this combined with the prospect of nationalization, drove a number of Cuban cigar manufacturers – many American-owned – to look for an alternative location, and many settled on the Dominican Republic.

The Dominican Republic is located in the eastern two-thirds of the Caribbean island of Hispaniola, with Haiti in the west. Like Cuba, tobacco has been grown in the Dominican Republic for thousands of years, having been cultivated and smoked by the island's indigenous Taíno population. Also like Cuba, Hispaniola was discovered by Christopher Columbus in 1492, and the island was soon used as a base from which Spain seized control of much of Central and South America.

The Dominican Republic covers an area of around 48,500 square kilometres (19,000 square miles), and has a population of about 9 million people. Unsurprisingly, being Cuba's neighbour, the country's climate and soil are comparable to the larger island, and tobacco, initially for use in cigarettes, has been grown commercially here since the early 1900s. In the 1970s and 1980s when the second-largest city, Santiago, was opened as a free trade zone, cigar manufacturers who formerly produced their cigars in the Canary Islands moved to the Dominican Republic and began growing higher-grade Cuban-seed tobacco for use in cigars, and a number of cigar factories sprang up.

The Yaque Valley

Most of the 240,000 hectares (600,000 acres) of tobacco plantations can be found in the north-west, in the Santiago and Cibao valleys, with the very best site being the Yaque Valley, which starts near Santiago and runs for around 40

◀ *The Yaque Del Norte River valley, an area important to the Dominican Republic for livestock, tobacco, coffee and fruit farming.*

▲ *As can be seen from this map, tobacco cultivation in the Dominican Republic's is concentrated in one area, the Cibao Valley.*

kilometres (25 miles) northwest to the town of Esperanza. The valley has been compared favourably to Cuba's premium tobacco-growing region of Vuelta Abajo.

The Dominican Republic has seen a huge growth in tobacco cultivation in the last 25 years, and several major cigar producers have been attracted to the region not only for its climate and soil but also because of the more recent stable economic and political situation. General Cigar Company (which produces Partagás and Ramón Allones cigars, to name just two), Altadis USA (Romeo y Julieta and Montecristo cigars), Arturo Fuente and Davidoff, among others, all produce very successful cigars here (see Cigar Directory, for further information). Most of the tobacco grown is used as filler, notably the three varieties known as *piloto cubano*, which is derived from seeds from Vuelta Abajo, the native *olor dominicano*, which

is renowned for its subtle taste, and *san vicente*, which is a slightly lighter hybrid of *piloto cubano*. However, a number of innovative producers, notably Arturo Fuente, have established their own farms and have been experimenting with growing wrapper tobacco, often to great acclaim.

Cigar Country

With such huge investment from numerous cigar producers, and the fact that the Dominican Republic now exports over 350 million cigars each year, the country is now the world's leading producer of premium cigars and has rightly earned the name 'Cigar Country'. The careful crop management and innovative thinking of the country's cigar producers has seen 'DR' cigars receive accolade after accolade from cigar lovers around the world, and the future looks bright.

HONDURAS AND NICARAGUA

Following the US embargo of Cuba, many tobacco producers established factories not only in the Dominican Republic but also in the neighbouring Central American countries of Honduras and Nicaragua. In fact, tobacco had been cultivated in the region by the indigenous populations for thousands of years.

By the 1960s and 1970s, a number of US-owned tobacco growers had become firmly established in Honduras, mixing Cuban-seed tobacco with local varieties, and with them once-exclusively Cuban brands such as Punch, Belinda and Hoyo de Monterrey thrived outside Cuba. The 1980s, however, were less kind to the Honduran cigar trade. Not only were various regions of the country used as bases by US-backed Contras during their struggle with the Nicaraguan Sandinistas, which brought all sorts of disruption to tobacco production, but in the mid-1980s Honduras' tobacco crop was severely depleted by infestations of blue mould (*moho azúl*), to which Cuban-seed tobacco is particularly prone. Although the industry started to thrive once more in the early 1990s, the country was hit by Hurricane Mitch in 1998 and 70 per cent of all Honduran crops were wiped out. Fortunately, however, Honduran cigar reserves were sufficient to meet consumer demand, and the plantations are now fully restored.

Honduran tobacco

The country's main growing regions are the Jamastran Valley in the southeast, where the rich soil yields the country's highest-quality tobacco, the more centrally located Talanga Valley, and the plantations of the Santa Rosa de Copán municipality in the western highlands, where a tobacco trading post was established by the Spanish in 1765. As well as growing mostly Cuban-seed tobacco, Honduras is notable for its Connecticut Shade wrapper tobacco, sometimes referred to as 'Honduran Shade'. Cigars from Honduras tend to be strong and rich tasting, underlined by the use of Cuban-seed tobacco, and they are aimed at filling the niche in the market created by the Cuban embargo.

◄ *Tobacco produced in Honduras' plantations tends to be stronger than that cultivated in the Dominican Republic or Nicaragua.*

Nicaragua

The history of Nicaragua's tobacco and cigar industries in many ways resembles that of neighbouring Honduras. Again, Cuban exiles kick-started Nicaragua's cigar manufacturing, particularly with the arrival of the cigar manufacturer José Padrón in 1970. The 1970s saw Nicaragua produce some of the finest premium cigars in the world, notably the Joya de Nicaragua. But when the socialist Sandinistas came to power in 1979, many of the tobacco plantations and cigar factories were nationalized and seized by the government, just as they had been in Cuba. Like Honduras, Nicaragua then suffered from the ensuing ten-year civil war between the Sandinista government and the US-backed Contras – only worse. In fact much of the fighting took place around one of the main tobacco-growing areas, the northwestern region of Estelí. Tobacco plantations were destroyed or turned into minefields, and cigar factories and curing houses were converted for military use or destroyed. Again, like

▲ *The tobacco-growing regions of Honduras and Nicaragua. The Jalapa Valley is known for its tobacco, which is comparable to Cuba's finest.*

Honduras, Nicaraguan tobacco also suffered from both blue mould infestation and Hurricane Mitch, during which some parts of the country received a year's worth of rain in four days; the topsoil of entire fields was washed away completely, leaving bare rock.

Nicaraguan resurgence

Nicaragua's cigar production has now returned to Estelí, while farther north lies the Condega Valley, the second most important cigar-producing region. Finally, along the border with Honduras lies the Jalapa Valley, which, like the Honduran Jamastran Valley, produces Nicaragua's best tobacco and is often compared favourably with the rich tobacco from Cuba's Vuelta Abajo. Since the mid-1990s, Nicaragua is again producing and exporting some of the world's finest premium cigars.

CONNECTICUT PLANTATIONS

While the United States produces and consumes more cigars than any other nation in the world, the great majority of these are machine-rolled and don't fall into the premium, hand-rolled cigar category. However, one New England state has given the lie to the fact that premium tobacco grows only in tropical climates.

Although there are several thousand hectares of tobacco plantations in South Carolina, Virginia, Tennessee, Georgia and Kentucky, Connecticut is the only American state producing premium tobacco. Wild tobacco had been collected and smoked by Native Americans along the banks of the Connecticut River Valley long before the arrival of Columbus, and although tobacco smoking was made illegal in the state in the mid-seventeenth century, by the early nineteenth century, once smoking had become widely accepted, tobacco became a major source of revenue in Connecticut.

Connecticut Shade

Today, the plantations north of Hartford grow a Hazelwood strain of Cuban-seed tobacco under 3-metre/10-foot high gauze tents that provide shade from the sun – hence the name Connecticut Shade. During the early 1920s, when tobacco cultivation was at its height in the region, some 12, 500 hectares (31,000 acres) were set aside for growing tobacco, but following the drop in the popularity of cigars after World War II due to cheap cigarettes and growing concerns over the health effects of tobacco, that figure has fallen to around 1,000 hectares (2,500 acres).

The light golden colour and mild to medium taste, combined with the good elasticity of Connecticut Shade,

◄ *The fertile agricultural plain of the Connecticut River, where many of the region's farms, including its tobacco farms, are situated.*

▲ *A Connecticut farm worker, photographed in 1941, cultivates Shade tobacco, covered by 'fields' of cheesecloth to protect it from the sun.*

an essential characteristic for premium wrapper leaf, has made this wrapper one of the best-regarded in the world. However, the amount of work that goes into growing and drying Connecticut Shade (the drying uses carefully controlled heat from gas burners) has ensured that this is also one of the most expensive wrappers to produce, which in turn is reflected in the cost. Today's Connecticut wrappers are used in a number of top-selling premium cigars including Davidoff and Macanudo, some of which, such as the Macanudo Robust, also use as a binder another type of tobacco grown in Connecticut, Connecticut Broadleaf.

▼ *The Davidoff Classic range of cigars, such as the No. 2 shown here, utilize an elegant claro (light-coloured) Connecticut Shade wrapper.*

MEXICO, JAMAICA, COSTA RICA, ECUADOR

It would be ironic if Mexico did not have a tobacco industry, since the cultivation and use of tobacco can be traced back to the Maya civilization of the Yucatán Peninsula, southeast Mexico. While the history of tobacco in Jamaica, Costa Rica and Ecuador is not as long-lived, these countries also have established cigar-producing traditions.

Almost all of Mexico's tobacco for premium cigars is grown in the state of Veracruz, which runs along the Gulf of Mexico on the country's east coast. The northern region of the state is home to a number of plantations growing both filler tobacco and a local dark variety called *tobacco negro*, which is used for wrappers. Of greater

significance, however, are the plantations located about 150 kilometres (90 miles) southeast of Veracruz City in the San Andres Valley. Here the soil and climate are said to resemble closely that of the Vuelta Abajo area in Cuba, and the region is most famous for tobacco cultivated with seeds from Sumatra, which is used in both binders and wrappers. The seeds are said to have been brought over by Dutch tobacco growers who were forced out of Indonesia after World War II.

Like Cuba in the late 1990s, the sudden growth of the cigar trade, particularly in the United States, was accompanied by a falling-off in standards. The San Andres Valley region in Mexico saw a number of smaller cigar producers appearing 'overnight'. Many of the new manufacturers were inexperienced. The drop in the overall quality of cigars exported to the United States resulted in Mexico's sales to that country falling from 25 million cigars in 1997 to 2.5 million in 2004. With the recent fall in demand, Mexico's more experienced manufacturers

◀ *A Jamaican tobacco seller in the 1920s, selling lengths of tobacco in Kingston. Jamaica's cigar industry grew after the US embargo of Cuba.*

▲ Rows of tobacco are hung out to dry on a farm in Tuxpan, in the Veracruz region of Mexico. Almost all of Mexico's premium tobacco is grown in this region.

are convinced that the quality of their cigars will become more consistent and that their reputation will be restored.

Jamaica

Although rarely thought of as a major cigar-producing country, Jamaica's tobacco plantations date back to the mid-seventeenth century when the island was a British colony. Much of the country's cigar production occurs around the capital, Kingston, and the cigars gained popularity in the United States following the Cuban embargo. During the 1980s, Jamaica's cigar industry grew to assume the position formerly held by the Canary Islands, as the major exporter of premium cigars to the United States. However, following the end of the boom years demand for premium cigars fell, resulting in factory closures, and in 2000 the General Cigar Company, which had been manufacturing cigars in Jamaica since 1968, moved its operation to the Dominican Republic.

Jamaica's tobacco plants are derived from Cuban, Dominican, Mexican and Honduran seeds, with wrapper leaves from Connecticut, Brazil and Indonesia.

Costa Rica

Although better known for its coffee plantations, Costa Rica's tobacco growing and cigar manufacturing expanded following Hurricane Mitch, which devastated much of the industry in Honduras and Nicaragua in 1998.

Ecuador

Ecuador's warm and humid tropical climate lends itself perfectly to tobacco growing, and the country now produces highly sought-after wrappers. Grown from both Sumatran and Connecticut seeds, they are famous for their silky texture and fine-veined structure, which is due to the cloud that covers much of the country's tobacco-growing regions, providing ideal natural shade.

OTHER TOBACCO-GROWING COUNTRIES

There are other tobacco-growing nations around the world, some on their way up, and others for whom the glory days are over. Although production pales into insignificance compared with Cuban, Dominican, Honduran or Nicaraguan cigar production, such countries are often renowned for creating unique and characteristic tobacco and cigars.

Most of the tobacco grown in Brazil comes from the state of Bahia, on the central east coast of the country. Here the local *mata fina* variety is the most common type of tobacco grown. Used as both a filler and a wrapper in a variety of well-received premium cigars, it's a dark tobacco rich in flavour that provides a full, yet smooth, smoking experience and which over the years has grown in popularity, particularly in the North American market.

▲ *A woman sorts through the dried tobacco leaves in a factory in San Felix, Brazil. Brazilian tobacco has been used as filler, binder and wrapper in a number of well-established premium cigar brands.*

Cameroon

Most plantations of this central west African country are found in the Bertoua region, in the east of the country and near the border with the neighbouring Central African Republic (which has a growing tobacco industry in its own right). Both countries grow a Sumatran-seed leaf known as Cameroon wrapper, which is used in a number of cigars produced by some of the most famous cigar makers in the world including H. Upmann, Ashton and Arturo Fuente. Cameroon leaf is green-brown to dark-brown in colour and is often referred to as 'toothy' due to the unique shape of

◀ *A tobacco manufacturer's sign in Tenerife. Gran Canaria, Tenerife and La Palma are the Canaries' main cigar manufacturing islands.*

the leaf's grain. As a wrapper, the leaf's neutral flavour ensures it complements perfectly more robust and full-flavoured fillers and binders.

Indonesia and the Philippines

The archipelago of Indonesia is home to the islands of Sumatra, Java and Borneo, all of which grow tobacco. Sumatra and Java are the sources of the wrapper leaves widely known as Sumatra- or Java-seed. Now cultivated around the world, the Sumatra-seed is recognized as the better of the two. On Borneo a filler tobacco known as 'Dutch flavour' is grown, the 'Dutch' referring to the legacy of Dutch colonization. The Sumatra-seed wrapper leaf is dark brown, silky to the touch and with a neutral flavour, while the Java-seed is similar but less consistent in quality.

The Philippines, Indonesia's neighbour, is one of the largest tobacco-producing countries in Asia and has a long history of cigar production dating back to the nineteenth century, when Manila cigars were considered to be on a par even with the great Havanas. That reputation has dwindled somewhat, and today the country produces an aromatic yet mild-tasting hybrid strain of tobacco.

Canary Islands

The Canary Islands, now the only location of hand-made cigars in Europe, have a long relationship with tobacco and cigars. Many people from the islands settled in Cuba during the early years of Spain's colonial rule in the Caribbean, and then conversely, following the introduction of the Cuban embargo in 1962, cigar makers such as the Menendez and Garcia families (responsible for the success of H. Upmann)

▲ A tobacco warehouse of the Compania General de Tobaccos de Philippines, established in 1881. It is still the leading cigar producer in the Philippines.

moved to the islands. During the 1960s and 1970s, the islands were the major exporter of cigars to the United States, featuring brands such as Montecruz. However, during the 1980s Cuban tobacco imports started to dry up and labour became increasingly expensive. Canary Island cigars in turn became overpriced and gained a reputation for inconsistency.

Most tobacco cultivation is situated on La Palma, the westernmost island. Here filler tobacco is grown in the eastern highlands of Breña Alta and blended with Cuban tobacco to make cigars, but in the cigar world the domestic crop is thought of quite poorly and a lack of investment sees the industry facing challenging times.

NON-CUBAN
OR CUBAN?

With the US embargo of Cuba still in place at time of writing, today's global premium (by which is meant entirely hand-made) cigar market can broadly be thought of in terms of the United States and 'the rest of the world', or non-Cuban versus Cuban.

◀ *A display of cigars in the H. Upmann factory in Havana, Cuba. H. Upmann is just one of many famous brands that exist both in Cuba and the Dominican Republic.*

Republic. Similarly, another household brand name (at least in a cigar-smoking household), Hoyo de Monterrey, is produced in both Cuba and Honduras. So how can one brand exist in two different places? Well, of course, again it's due to the US embargo. When Fidel Castro nationalized the privately owned Cuban cigar businesses, he seized control not only of the factories and warehouses but also the brand names of the cigars that the factories produced. Meanwhile, those Cuban cigar families who fled from Castro and Cuba took with them their years – in most cases generations – of experience, knowledge of tobacco blending and rolling, and their brands, and set up business in the other regions we've been considering. Even today, after 45 years of the embargo, there are still numerous unresolved intellectual property rights' cases. Later in the book we'll tell you what to look for to indicate what you're buying, but for now, remember that most brands made in Cuba will have 'Habana' written somewhere on the label.

As alluded to earlier, one of the most confusing aspects of the premium cigar market, particularly for non-aficionados, is that there appear to be a number of 'Cuban' brands produced outside Cuba in countries such as the Dominican Republic, Honduras, Nicaragua and so forth (and often with wrappers from a different country of origin than the binders and fillers). For example, you'll find one of the most famous brands, H. Upmann, deriving from both Cuba and the Dominican

Thanks Fidel!

In many ways, without Fidel, the Cuban Revolution and the seizure of the cigar factories, we might never have heard of a Dominican Montecristo or a Honduran Punch. It seems unlikely that the Cuban cigar barons would ever have bothered to try growing Cuban-seed tobacco anywhere outside Cuba or been forced to experiment creating cigars with wrappers from West Africa, filler from the Dominican Republic and the binder from the United States. So in many ways the cigar lover has a great deal to be thankful for to Fidel. Cigar producers have been made to think creatively and innovatively to ensure that they can provide the best possible cigars with the raw materials available. But that's not to say that the raw materials outside Cuba are necessarily inferior to those within Cuba. In fact, as any magazine that reviews and rates cigars will demonstrate, many non-Cuban cigars have often 'outperformed' those from Cuba – just as many New World wines have fared better in blind tastings than those from France. As with anything to do with taste – whether wine, whisky or cigars – there are no hard and fast rules: it's simply down to personal subjective preference.

▲ *Fidel Castro with Compay Segundo, the famous Cuban singer, at the 2001 Havana Cigar Festival.*

Post embargo

It's impossible to second-guess what will happen to the cigar industry if and when the US embargo is lifted. There's bound to be a surge in interest from the United States in Cuban cigars, and it's likely that the Cuban manufacturers will be tempted to overcook productivity (as they did in the late 1990s). However, many of the Cuban manufacturers are aware of the mistakes made in the late 1990s, and the effect they had on long-term sales (and the Cuban reputation), and so when the time comes it is hoped they will increase production in a controlled and stable manner. But it seems unlikely that the now highly successful and lucrative 45-year-old, non-Cuban cigar market will disappear overnight. One prospect that many aficionados will be looking forward to is more innovative blends of tobacco, only this time with Cuban varieties included.

◀ *Most Cuban brands will have 'Habana' written on the label, as on the label on this box of Vegas Robaina cigars.*

THE 'BOOM YEARS' 1993–97 AND BEYOND

An extraordinary thing happened to the premium cigar market in the United States between 1993 and 1997, which to a certain extent was mirrored in Europe. During that time cigar retailers in America experienced sales growth of 20 per cent or more, in an industry that historically would have been satisfied with a steady one or two per cent in the same period.

◀ *Martin Shanker, founder of the popular magazine* Cigar Aficionado, *in his humidor room, 1994.*

While it's difficult to understand exactly why there was such a fast-growing demand for premium cigars from 1993 to 1997, we can at least look back on the effects with the benefit of hindsight. During that period the entire cigar industry in the United States experienced some quite radical changes. The surge in interest and demand for 'big' or 'wet' cigars (as the industry often refers to premium cigars) saw an entirely new group of people – from consumers through to retailers and manufacturers – enter into a business that they knew very little about. Some observers felt that the established manufacturers realized they could make much more money selling 'super premium' new brands at inflated prices than they could selling the established brands at standard prices – which would explain the sudden chronic shortage of the old brands.

So why did American premium cigar imports increase from around 120 million in 1993 to over 500 million in 1997? Many have put it down to one magazine, *Cigar Aficionado*, which was first launched in September 1992. Although it seems unlikely that one magazine could be responsible for creating such phenomenal growth, there's no doubt that the magazine certainly hit the right chord and helped to sell a great deal of cigars. Whether the result of one magazine or not, cigars were suddenly trendy and hip, and more and more people were smoking them; we'll be taking a closer look at the cult of the cigar on pages 52–53.

Europe and Cuba

Whether influenced by profiteering or not, there was also a shortage of established brand names because Europe, itself experiencing steady growth in cigar sales, was becoming increasingly dissatisfied with the quality of the cigars from an overstretched and under-resourced Cuba. Europe was also developing a taste for the milder cigars from the Dominican Republic and elsewhere.

Post-boom

These reasons, combined with the fact that an increasingly diverse portfolio of retailers began to jump on the cigar bandwagon, meant that the honest, well-established tobacconist was unable to supply regular customers with their favourite brands, and the crop of new 'super premium' brands available seemed overpriced and, frankly, not that 'super'. Fortunately for the discerning cigar

▲ *It would seem that modern-day trips to Cuba would not be complete without buying cigars, even for non-aficionados.*

enthusiast, by 1997–98 the fad was over and the cigar industry settled down. Although this resulted in factory closures and bankrupt retailers, it meant that the name brands were once more readily available, back orders were being filled and the general quality of cigars improved. So where does that leave us today?

▼ *Tony Curtis, Milton Berle and two Playboy bunnies at the Friar's Club in Beverly Hills, California in 1998.*

GLOBAL TRADE TODAY

Although there was a distinct dip in the cigar trade following the end of the 'boom' years in 1997, which was most pronounced in the United States – Europe and the rest of the world remaining relatively stable – by 2002 production standards and quality control gradually started to improve.

◀ A young girl sits beside a cigar booth outside a bar on Calle O'Reilly, Havana, Cuba. The cigars are priced in US dollars.

Despite an increasing number of countries introducing anti-smoking legislation, many industry insiders feel that the premium cigar market is now in quite good shape, both in the United States and the rest of the world. In 2004 some companies were achieving sales figures that outstripped those from the boom years, and many spokesmen and commentators were referring to a 'mini-boom'. Whether they are proved right only time will tell, but there is a general feeling among the cigar producers that stable rather than booming growth is good for them and good for the consumer. It allows the producers to plan ahead and maintain strict quality control both in terms of their tobacco (which is bought and then matured for two or more years before being used to make cigars) and the cigar manufacturing process. Many cigar producers suffered from poor quality control during the boom period in a bid to meet demand, and their reputations suffered. Many are now saying that even if there were another boom they would avoid the temptation of increasing output at the risk of compromising quality.

Cuba

Although not directly involved with the booming American market during the mid-1990s, Cuba experienced a situation similar to other cigar-producing nations and, as already mentioned, the quality of Cuban cigars suffered; at one point during the late 1990s Habanos S.A., the company responsible for marketing and selling all Cuban cigars abroad, was promoting the idea that Cuba could produce 300 million cigars a year, which is almost twice the number the country is presently producing. Such an inflated figure was rapidly revised down to 250 and then 200 million. Based on the present amount of land set aside for tobacco cultivation, it is doubtful that even that figure would ever have

▲ *Cigar manufacturer Altadis S.A. has developed a new variety of tobacco, which has leaves resistant to blue mould.*

been achievable, particularly given the poor state of Cuba's economy following the collapse of the Soviet Union in 1991, combined with the effect of poor harvests following a spate of hurricanes. But with cigars bringing in desperately needed foreign currency, it's understandable that Cuba would be tempted to increase productivity as far as possible.

Altadis

The Cuban cigar industry was thrown a lifeline in February 2000, when the giant European tobacco company Altadis S.A. paid $500 million for a 50 per cent stake in Habanos S.A. This enabled Habanos to buy much-needed fertilizer for tobacco farmers, to upgrade production methods and generally do business in a much more economically stable environment.

The future looks very bright for Cuba. Many experts are saying that the quality of the cigars is now equal to the previous high standards, if not better. The introduction of a variety of tobacco called Habana 2000, which is much more resistant to blue mould, will also help to ensure that tobacco harvests are consistently excellent: all in all the news is good for all lovers of Cuban cigars.

◄ *A box of 2006 Cohíba Behike. These Cuban cigars cost $440 each and come in boxes of 40. They are among the most expensive cigars sold.*

THE CULT OF THE CIGAR

The cult of the cigar really hit its stride at the end of the nineteenth century in both Europe and the United States. But as with all relatively new fashions it required high-profile advocates for the rest of society to follow. Today's aficionados have these early cigar ambassadors to thank.

◀ Cigar makers in Little Havana sued the cigar-loving rapper P. Diddy for allegedly revealing secret cigar-rolling techniques in one of his music videos.

Cigars and the famous

Winston Churchill smoked about ten cigars a day and his name was given to the large corona-format cigar. Of course America also had its share of fine cigar ambassadors who helped popularize the early cause of the cigar – the most famous being Ulysses S. Grant, the American Civil War Union general and the eighteenth president of the United States. But in fact Grant's love of cigars was somewhat thrust upon him. Before the Civil War (1861–65) Grant was an occasional smoker only, but when a photo of him smoking a cigar was published following a victorious battle during which he won the nickname 'Unconditional Surrender' Grant, well-wishers and supporters inundated him with cigars.

It's alleged that soon after the vehemently anti-smoking Queen Victoria died in 1901, her son and the new king Edward VII said to his male guests after finishing dinner, 'Gentlemen, you may proceed to smoke.' Edward, after whom the popular machine-made 'King Edward' cigars are named, was a cigar lover – smoking 12 large cigars a day. Maybe it could be said that this was the beginning of the cult of the cigar and cigars were soon popular with entertainers, writers, politicians, musicians and sportsmen.

But Grant's cigar smoking pales to insignificance compared with another early advocate – the author and journalist Samuel Clemens, more commonly known by his pen name Mark Twain. Clemens smoked his first cigar when he was eight – after which he was soon smoking 100 cigars a month. 'Before I was thirty I had increased it to three hundred a month', he continued

▶ *Cigar lover Samuel Clemens (the real name of the American writer Mark Twain) wrote that 'if Heaven has no cigars, I shall not go there'.*

in his 1883 essay 'Smoking as Inspiration'. Clemens' cigar smoking, which began first thing in the morning and ended last thing at night, unsurprisingly placed a huge strain on his marriage to his wife Olivia.

There are numerous cigar-touting musicians, from jazz virtuosos such as Miles Davis to rap and hip hop stars such as P. Diddy. Arthur Rubinstein, one of the greatest classical pianists of the twentieth century, was a devoted cigar aficionado.

Gastronomic cigars

Of course it is not only the rich and famous who enjoy a good cigar. Many of us enjoy smoking cigars after consuming a fine meal. A post-prandial cigar can be enjoyed following almost any type of cuisine, from spicy Asian food to Continental cuisine, although Chinese food doesn't tend to set the palate up for an after-dinner cigar. The two drinks most commonly associated with cigar smoking are port and brandy, though Scotch and bourbon and various liqueurs are also suitable companions. However, if you fancy something less strong, wine and even certain lagers, beers and stouts go well with cigars. And, if you want to avoid alcohol altogether, a good strong espresso will provide you with the perfect cigar partner.

And, despite the increasingly widespread legislation against smoking in public, it seems that people will still be able to enjoy the odd smoke in the

◀ *Comedian Groucho Marx rarely appeared on or off screen without a cigar. He famously quipped 'Given the choice between a woman and a cigar, I will always choose the cigar.'*

2

THE ANATOMY
OF CIGARS

SOWING AND GROWING

Tobacco plants are grown in one of two ways – sun grown or shade grown. Sun-grown tobacco is fully exposed to direct sunlight throughout the growing season, and will be darker and stronger in flavour. However, some sun-grown tobacco, particularly that from Indonesia, can be relatively mild due to constant cloud cover.

◄ *Farmers plant tobacco seedlings in Vinales, Cuba. Surrounded by limestone hills, the fertile Vinales Valley produces tobacco for Cuba's finest cigars.*

plant, and much of Cuba's production was lost in the early years of the US embargo due to a lack of fertilizer, among other things. The fields are then ploughed in preparation for sowing. The preparation of the tobacco fields varies from country to country and from plantation to plantation, with some more mechanized than others. In Cuba, the traditional ox and plough are still commonly used. This is partly due to a lack of fossil fuels and spare parts for tractors, but also because many growers believe that tractors damage the land by compacting it. Sowing times also vary from country to country depending on their particular climate, but in Cuba the seedlings can be transplanted any time between mid-October and mid-January, depending on the seed variety and the weather conditions.

Shade-grown tobacco is grown under muslin-like material that cuts out about 30 per cent of the sunlight. The purpose of the shade is not so much to affect the flavour of the tobacco as to ensure that the leaves are kept free from all blemishes. The resulting leaves are milder tasting and paler in colour than the sun-grown type.

Like all plants, the tobacco plant begins life as a seed – each seed being the size of a grain of sand. Having germinated in greenhouses, the seeds are sown into soil seedbeds, or more recently into seed trays, where they remain for a further six weeks. When the seeds have reached around 15–20 centimetres (6–8 inches) in height, the healthiest seedlings are transplanted into the tobacco fields. Before the seedlings are transplanted the tobacco fields are fed with fertilizer; tobacco is an extremely hungry

Cultivation

Cultivating the plants is an elaborate and time-consuming task. Four to five days after the initial transplantation, the fields are watered and any dead seedlings are replaced with new plants to ensure that the fields produce the maximum yield. This process is repeated after a further four to five days. During the early stages of the growing season, the farmers regularly use cultivators to remove weeds between the rows of tobacco plants, and to loosen and break up the soil. Between 18 and 20 days after the initial transplantation the soil is then gently piled around the young plants by workers using hoes in a process known as 'earthing up'. This helps the plants' roots to develop and creates irrigation ditches to ensure any excess rainwater is washed away. Fertilizer is usually applied to the plants at three key stages. First, as mentioned above, before the seedlings are initially sown; a second application takes place when the fields are cultivated to remove weeds; and the third during earthing up.

Irrigation

Judging levels of irrigation is an important skill that tobacco farmers must learn. Shade- and sun-grown tobacco require different amounts of irrigation; shade-grown tobacco requires more water as this helps to produce large leaves with clear and uniform colours and a mild flavour, ideal for wrappers. However, too much water applied to sun-grown tobacco can take away the strong aromas required for filler leaf. Generally most watering occurs during transplantation and harvesting; if the leaves don't receive sufficient water around the time they are harvested, they won't cure properly.

Pinching out and suckering

Another key process is 'pinching out', which takes place 38–42 days after planting. During pinching out the vegetative tissue that forms the bud of the plant is removed. This redirects the plant's energy away from reproduction into leaf growth, thereby improving the yield. Each individual plant must be pinched out by hand, and judging when to pinch out and exactly which parts of the plant should be removed takes years of experience. Soon after pinching out, the plant will quickly develop new shoots called 'suckers'. These must also be removed or else they too will re-divert valuable energy away from the leaves into new growth.

▼ *A Cuban farmer harvests tobacco by hand in a field near Pinar del Río. Eighty per cent of Cuba's tobacco comes from this region.*

HARVESTING

There are three principal ways in which tobacco is harvested, and these apply to most of the world's tobacco-growing regions. The first is in stages, often referred to as priming; the second is stalk-cut, in which the entire plant is harvested at once; and the third is a combination of the first two.

All shade-grown and some sun-grown tobacco is harvested in stages by hand, following a strict sequence that relates to the position of the leaves on the plant and at what stage they reach maturity. In general terms the stages, or primings, run as follows:

• First priming, or *libre de pie* (at the base), takes place 45–50 days after sowing, and involves removing the lowest two or three leaves nearest the ground. These leaves tend to be light and sweet, and are most commonly used as binders because they burn smoothly and evenly. They are also used as fillers or occasionally as wrappers.

• Second priming, or *uno y medio* (one-and-a-half), takes place 50–52 days after sowing, during which two leaves are normally taken from each plant. These leaves are still sweet but have a slightly higher nicotine content, making them fuller flavoured.

Again, second-priming leaves are used primarily for binders and fillers.

• Third priming, or *centro ligero* (light centre), takes place 58–62 days after sowing. The two to four high-quality leaves taken from each plant have more robust flavours than those of the second priming, are most often used as wrappers, but are also used to balance other filler leaves.

• Fourth priming, or *centro fino* (thin centre), takes place 68–72 days after sowing, and the leaves are considered the highest quality. Again, two to four leaves are taken from each plant, and their rich flavour and darker colour make them well suited as both wrappers and fillers.

▼ *A farmer harvests tobacco leaves in Wisconsin, USA.*

• Fifth priming, or *centro gordo* (thick centre), takes place 73–75 days after sowing. The two leaves collected from each plant are thick and dark, and contain the most oils and resins. Their strong flavour requires longer fermentation than the previous leaves and they are ideal for use as either fillers or binders, but occasionally as wrappers.

• Sixth priming, or *corona* (crown), takes place 75–80 days after sowing, and equates to the top two leaves of the plant. These leaves tend to be aged the longest (up to five years) because they are the most powerfully flavoured. Corona leaves are mostly too small to use as wrappers. The high quality of shade leaf

▲ *A farmer cuts tobacco in Tennessee, USA. Many farmers in Tennessee depend solely on their small plots of tobacco for their income.*

often benefits from additional primings, known as *primer centro ligero* (first light centre), *segundo centro ligero* (second light centre), *primer centro fino* (first thin centre) and *segundo centro fino* (second thin centre).

Stalk-cut and mixed harvesting

Stalk-cut plants provide tobacco of slightly lower quality, as the leaves are harvested all at once and therefore are not necessarily at their optimum level of maturity. Mixed harvesting involves removing the lower leaves 40–50 days after sowing, and then harvesting the remainder of the plant when it has reached maturity after 75–80 days.

CURING AND FERMENTATION

To facilitate the curing process, the harvested leaves are 'strung' onto smooth twine using large needles, which are passed through the thickest part of the leaf's midrib. Around 120–200 leaves are strung onto one length of twine and hung over a pole. The poles are hung horizontally in curing sheds so air can circulate through the leaves.

It's important to note that curing differs from drying in a number of key aspects. Drying is simply the evaporation of water from the leaves, and although this is an integral part of the curing process, it is only one element. In curing, during which the leaf's cells remain active for three to five days, the leaves also undergo complex chemical and biological changes, many of which

▼ *A tobacco drying house in Viñales, Cuba. It is the drying process that gives the tobacco its distinctive flavour and aroma.*

involve decomposition and the production of certain enzymes. The most visually apparent aspect of curing occurs when the green chlorophyll in the leaves starts to turn to a yellowy-brown carotene, giving the leaves their majestic earthy colour.

Air curing

To work effectively, curing relies on three factors: temperature, humidity and the circulation of air. The most common form of curing in Cuba and most other Caribbean tobacco-growing regions is air curing. Air curing occurs in wooden barns deliberately built along an east-west axis – the theory being that one end of the barn is heated in the morning and the other in the afternoon. The barns also have doors or openings at each end and

▲ The harvested tobacco is tied into bundles ready for fermentation. It is then hung over wooden poles in a drying barn known as a secadero.

along the sides, which allows a certain amount of control over the temperature, humidity and air circulation.

Air curing takes anywhere between 40 and 60 days (depending on the weather conditions), and occurs during the warmest time of the year. One of the main drawbacks to air curing is that the leaves need to be moist in order to loosen the leaves from the string, and so the producers often have to wait until it has rained before they can collect the leaves together.

Flue curing

Another method of curing, and one that has become increasingly widespread in Cuba in recent years, particularly for curing wrapper leaf, is flue curing. This process relies on the same three factors as air curing – temperature, humidity and air circulation – but it occurs in a much more controlled environment, namely an enclosed barn that has heated flues running through it. The temperature of the flues is controlled to ensure that temperature and humidity in the barn are at optimum values. Controlling the

environment within the barn helps speed up the curing process, which, using this method, takes between 20 and 25 days.

Fermentation

Once the leaves have been cured, they are taken down from the poles and loosened (ideally when humidity is high), and bundled together to form sheaves around 1 metre (3 feet) long. They are then taken to the area of the curing barn that is set aside for the primary fermentation process. The leaves will undergo another period of fermentation once they have been stripped and sorted into wrappers, fillers and binders.

During primary fermentation, which lasts between 35 and 40 days, any remaining sugars and starches are broken down, the leaves continue to darken and become more uniform in colour, oxidation occurs, and a rich aroma begins to make itself increasingly apparent. During the process the piles of leaves naturally reach temperatures as high as 33.3°C (92°F). To keep the temperatures constant and to ensure that all the tobacco is fermented, the piles are often broken up and turned over, as many as six times. Primary fermentation is completed when the temperature becomes more uniform.

SORTING AND STRIPPING

Once the tobacco leaves are fully fermented, they are collected together into bundles and taken to the next stage of the journey – the sorting house, or *escogida*. Sorting houses are found either near the plantations in the country or in towns, and it's here that the tobacco undergoes some of the final production procedures.

The main function of the sorting house is to continue the long and painstaking selection process to ensure that leaves of comparable colour, size, texture and grade are sorted together. To begin with, the fermented bundles are broken open and the leaves shaken apart in order to separate them. Once separated, the leaves are then carried in baskets to a moistening room, where they are subjected to a very fine spray of water before being aired on wooden racks and set aside for sorting the following day. The moistening process makes the leaves easier to handle and less likely to tear.

Wrappers

The strictest selection processes are reserved for the wrappers. In the sorting house wrapper leaves are divided into *ligero* (light), *seco* (dry), *viso* (glossy), *amarillo* (yellow) and *medio tempo* (half time, ie, leaves from the top half of the plant). If the harvest has been good, the leaves can often be further subdivided into *ligero seco*, *ligero viso seco* and so on. Any torn or broken wrappers will be discarded and used in cigarettes. Fillers and binders are also separated out by size and flavour.

After the wrappers have been sorted and graded, they are formed into bunches of 40–50 leaves, tied together at one end. The leaves are then carried in baskets to an area where they are allowed to rest, before being baled and stored in a warehouse where they age for between one and five years. Unlike binder and filler leaves, wrapper leaves don't usually undergo a second fermentation process. This is because wrapper leaves have a milder taste (due to many being shade-grown), and they don't therefore need

◀ *Workers load bales of tobacco leaves at the Partagás cigar factory. The leaves are taken to a warehouse and stored for between one and five years.*

▲ *Tobacco leaves are sorted at La Corona cigar factory in Havana. The leaves are sorted depending on intended purpose, colour, size and quality.*

a second fermentation to remove any residual bitterness that may be left in filler or binder. However, some cigar producers, such as J.C. Newman, do use wrapper leaves that have been fermented twice, claiming that the process provides a uniquely smooth, sweet flavour.

Binders and fillers

Meanwhile, the binder and filler leaves are sent to a stripping house, where they are again moistened if necessary, to make them more manageable to complete the highly skilled process of stripping the central midrib out of the leaf. After the leaves have been stripped, they are flattened between wooden boards and sent to a fermentation room, where they are formed into 2-metre- (6-foot) high piles, or *burros*. The second fermentation process varies in length depending on the leaf type – 90 days for *ligero*, 60 days for *seco* and 45 days for *volado*. After the leaves have been air dried, they are baled and wrapped in palm bark and sent to the warehouse or factory, where the leaves age for anything between one and three years.

▶ *A worker selects and sorts tobacco leaves in a Havana cigar factory according to size, colour, texture and quality.*

THE ANATOMY OF A CIGAR

Before we continue with the next cigar production processes, such as blending, rolling and banding, let's look more closely at the object itself. A cigar is made up of many constituent parts, each playing a vital role in delivering the tobacco that is so painstakingly cultivated, cured, sorted and fermented as smoothly and as evenly as possible.

◀ *Unbroken, long filler leaf is at the heart of all premium, hand-rolled cigars. On the bench is a* media ruedas *of 50 cigars.*

W e know that there are three main tobacco elements in each premium, hand-rolled cigar – the filler, the binder and the wrapper – and the leaves that make up each of those three elements are selected specifically to fulfil that role.

Filler

The filler is the heart of the cigar. It gives it most of its characteristic flavour and strength. In all good premium cigars the filler is made up of unbroken leaf, usually referred to as 'long filler'. As we know, there are three types of filler – *ligero* (from the top part, or corona, of the plant and the most flavourful filler), *seco* (from the middle part of the plant, and lighter than *ligero* in both colour and flavour), and *volado* (from the lowest third of the plant, and used primarily for its combustion properties). The filler is usually constructed with the strong *ligero* leaf in the centre, the lighter *seco* leaf around the *ligero*, and the *volado* surrounding both the *ligero* and *seco*.

The three different types of filler are carefully folded, or 'bunched', rather like the way an accordion closes together. If you look down the end of a premium cigar, you should always be able to see the way the filler is folded in on itself. This is important as it affects the way the cigar draws.

Binder

Wrapped around the filler is the binder, or *capote* which, as its name suggests, binds the filler leaves together. The binder leaf, although not adding much in terms of taste, should complement the filler's strength and flavour, as well as provide tensile strength.

Wrapper

The wrapper is the outermost leaf of the cigar, and while everyone agrees that wrapper leaves are cultivated and selected for their appearance and elasticity, views differ about how much flavour they give to a cigar. In Cuba, for example, most people consider that the filler provides the cigar with almost all its taste characteristics, while the wrapper provides only a 'top note'. In other countries, such as the Dominican Republic, the wrapper is believed to provide at least

▲ A cigar roller prepares the filler leaves by folding them like a fan. Called an accordion fold, it ensures that the cigar draws well.

half the cigar's flavour. Either way, the extraordinary amount of time, expertise, equipment and effort that go into creating wrapper leaves ensure that they are the single most expensive raw ingredient of a premium cigar.

To ensure that the wrapper leaf doesn't unravel, a cap made out of discarded wrapper is fixed to the end of the cigar. This is the part of the cigar that has to be cut off before it is ready to smoke.

▶ A cigar's cap stops the wrapper leaf from unravelling. A rounded (rather than pointed) cap is usually a sign of a hand-made cigar.

CREATING A CIGAR

The mystique surrounding cigar rollers, or *torcedores* and *torcedoras*, is legendary; many of them pass down the secrets of their skill from generation to generation. Rolling cigars is an art, and one that takes years to perfect. In Cuba, for example, there are several grades of roller, and reaching the highest grade can take up to ten years.

1 The aged and mature tobacco is unpacked and sorted, and if necessary, remoistened before being taken to the factory's blending room. Here the master blender, using 'recipe' books that detail the precise filler blend for the cigars that are going to be rolled that day, gathers together the necessary tobacco, which is then distributed to the rollers.

2 The roller begins by stretching a binder leaf flat on the table, into which the filler leaves are collected. The filler leaves are folded together like a fan to ensure the cigar draws well. The roller then wraps the binder around the filler to form a 'bunch'. The bunch is trimmed to the appropriate length (depending on the type of cigar) using a semicircular cutter or blade, the *chaveta*.

3 The bunch is placed into the bottom half of a mould. Traditionally the moulds were made of wood, but an increasing number of cigar factories around the world are now using plastic moulds. The size of the mould dictates the eventual ring gauge (circumference) of the cigar. The top half of the mould is placed over the bottom.

4 Several enclosed moulds are placed together under a press for 45–60 minutes. The press is released once or twice for the roller to turn the bunches to ensure they are evenly moulded into a perfect cylinder. In larger, more mechanized factories, the bunches may well be placed on sucking machines that check the draw. Any bunches that fail are returned to the roller, who dismantles them before reassembling and pressing them again. Satisfactory bunches are ready to be wrapped.

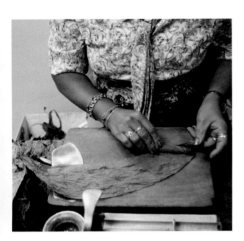

5 The wrapper leaves are often soaked overnight to regain their elasticity and to stop them from breaking up when being handled. Before being rolled, if necessary the wrapper is stripped and then laid 'face down' on the roller's desk so that any remaining evidence of the leaf's veins will be hidden. The roller cuts the wrapper to an appropriate size and places the bunch diagonally in the centre of the cut wrapper. The bunch is then rolled in the wrapper.

6 The wrapper is stuck down with a vegetable gum, and the excess trimmed. A small piece of discarded wrapper is affixed to one end to form the cap. The open end is then trimmed and the circumference checked to ensure the cigar is the correct length and has the right ring gauge.

On average it takes an experienced roller between four and five minutes to roll a cigar (not including pressing time), and therefore each roller can expect to roll around 120 cigars a day.

QUALITY CONTROL

Although the rollers make every effort to ensure that their cigars are of the highest possible standard, premium cigars are sometimes flawed; the process of rolling a premium cigar is, after all, entirely manual and mistakes will happen. To keep the number of flawed cigars to a minimum, they undergo rigorous quality-control checks.

◀ *Bundles of cigars before grading. Each roller ties his cigars into bundles of 50. A sample is taken from each roller and tested in eight categories.*

Each roller gathers together bundles of 50 of his or her newly rolled cigars – known as *media ruedas*, literally 'half wheels' – and ties a coloured ribbon around each. The colour of the ribbon is unique to the *torcedor(a)*. Alternatively, rather than using ribbon, a small card with the roller's reference number and the time and date indicating when the cigars were rolled is inserted in each bundle. In some factories the bundles are then treated for potential pests by undergoing a short period of fumigation in a sealed chamber. The fumigation process doesn't affect the flavour of the cigars.

Random selections

After the cigars have been treated, a representative sample of each roller's output is taken to an area where a number

of checks is carried out. Most factories have about eight categories against which the cigars are measured, including length, ring gauge, consistency, neatness of the foot (the end of the cigar that is lit), and colour, texture and smoothness of the wrapper. Often bundles of cigars are weighed against set parameters, depending on the size and shape of the cigar. Because the rollers are so consistent in their work, if a bundle weighs more or less than it should, then there may be a problem. If the cigar is overweight, it may contain too much tobacco and therefore be difficult to draw; if the cigar is underweight, it may not contain enough tobacco and will burn too quickly and too hot, making the smoke taste bitter.

Blind tastings

After a sufficient number of cigars has passed through the controls outlined above, a few will be taken for a blind taste test. The tasters, or *cantadores/cantadoras*, taste only in the morning, smoking about an inch of each cigar. They usually grade the cigars on five criteria – draw, strength, aroma, combustion and

taste – with each criterion having around seven or eight levels. Notes are made about each cigar and handed back to a manager, who can check the batch code against the roller's name and advise him or her if there are any problems with the cigars. As rollers are paid for each cigar that passes the various tests, it's in their interest to roll to the best of their ability. It is not unknown for a roller's entire batch to be rejected, in which case he or she may lose a day or two's pay.

Automation

Outlined above are the traditional quality checks performed on cigars made in Cuba, and in other factories in the Caribbean that use Cuba as their model. However, an increasing number of factories in the Dominican Republic and elsewhere are becoming more automated in terms of quality control. As we've seen, many use sucking machines at various stages of

▲ *A factory worker tests the draw of a cigar on a machine in Honduras. Any cigars that fail the test are discarded.*

production to check on the cigar's draw, and it seems likely that more and more factories will install such machines. Other companies are switching from wooden to plastic moulds, which are thought to last longer and are less susceptible to wear and tear. No doubt there'll be more mechanical innovations in the premium cigar business in the future, but it's unlikely that any will ever truly replace the experienced hands of the cigar roller.

▼ *Cigars are examined at the La Aurora cigar factory in the Dominican Republic. The inspector checks the overall look and feel of a random selection of cigars.*

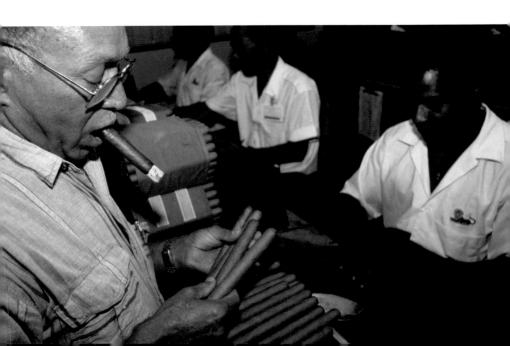

CONDITIONING AND COLOUR GRADING

After the bundles have been through quality control, they are ready for the last few packaging stages before being shipped to their final destinations. By this time it is estimated that each cigar will have undergone around 200 different stages – from sowing and growing to sorting and rolling, with each stage requiring manual expertise.

◀ *Cuban cigars sit on shelves tied in bundles at the Montecristo cigar factory in Havana. The cards will carry details of the each bundle's* torcedor(a).

of tobacco used in the cigar to blend and marry together, and second, that any final fermentation can occur, thereby hopefully removing all traces of bitterness when the cigar is smoked.

Colour grading

After around three weeks in the *escaparates* (even longer for some super-premium cigars), the bundled cigars are graded by colour. Given that cigars can be graded into about 65 different hues, it's hardly surprising that the colour graders, or *escogedores/escogedoras*, are considered as skilful as the most experienced rollers and are paid similar wages.

Before the cigars are sent off to be boxed, they are first conditioned in large, specially designed cooling cabinets known as *escaparates*. The purpose of this final conditioning process is to dry off any moisture that the tobacco may have picked up in the cigar factory. For example, before rolling, some fillers and binders and most wrappers are moistened, often overnight, to make them more malleable. Two other important aspects of this final conditioning process are, first, that it allows the different types

The 65 different hues are broadly classified into five main groups:

• *Maduro* These are the darkest wrappers, being dark to very dark brown in colour. *Maduro* wrappers, although very dark in colour, can vary in taste from sweet (due to a longer fermentation period), through mellow, to strong earthy flavours. *Maduro*

is often considered the traditional colour of Cuban cigars. A very dark form of *maduro*, which is called *oscuro* and is almost black in colour, is occasionally used.

• *Colorado* These are dark reddish-brown wrappers, and although they often have a gentle aroma, they can taste quite strong, with some being relatively sweet.

• *Colorado claro* Also known as EMS (English Market Selection) wrappers, these sun-grown wrappers are light brown to brown in colour and are less robust than the *colorado* and *maduro*.

• *Claro* These are light, tan-coloured wrappers, usually made from shade-grown leaf. They have a mild, smooth flavour.

• Double *claro* This is a light-green wrapper (also called AMS – American Market Selection – or *candela*). With an extremely mild flavour, these wrappers were once very popular in America, but have now gone out of fashion.

▶ *A cigar quality inspector at work checks boxes of Larranaga cigars for flaws in wrapper colour, at a factory in Cuba.*

▲ *The* escogedoras *are responsible for colour grading the cigars, so that each finished box has wrapper leaves of almost identical colour.*

After the cigars have been meticulously colour graded, they are put into their cedar boxes. Although the cigars are meant to be as uniform as possible in colour, if there is any change in colour, you'll notice that they will have been positioned to progress from dark to light, running left to right. The cigars then have their distinctive bands put on, indicating their specific brand. The workers putting on the bands take the cigars out one by one so that the order of the cigars in the box remains unchanged.

BOXES, SEALS AND LABELS

Although most brands of premium cigars are available in aluminium tubes lined with cedar, the great majority are packaged in boxes of 25, 50 or even 100 cigars. The boxes are usually made out of cedar wood, which stops the cigars from drying out and also helps the maturing process and has a pleasant aroma of its own.

◄ *A genuine box of Cuban cigars has a code on the seal that shows up when the box is placed under ultraviolet light.*

The most popular size of cigar box contains 25 cigars in two layers – a row of 13 on the top and another of 12 on the bottom, including a wooden or cardboard stop that prevents the cigars from rolling about. Between the two layers is placed a thin sheet of cedar wood. The insides of the box are usually lined with thin, coloured paper, which then folds over to cover the cigar layers.

After the cigars have been checked one final time, the top of the box, which usually features a cloth hinge, is nailed down with a pin-like nail and any relevant stickers, such as country of origin, the date on which the cigars were boxed, and a manufacturer's code are stuck on. This type of box is often referred to as a flat-dressed, or nailed wood box, as the corners

are held together with small nails or pins. Such boxes are usually covered with paper on which is printed the manufacturer's unique decorative artwork.

Avoiding counterfeit cigars

Anywhere that sells cigars is a target for counterfeit Cuban cigars, because real ones are worth a lot of money. Before buying a box, the key is to look carefully at the box itself. There should be a 'Republica de Cuba' warranty seal stuck to the front left edge of flat-dressed boxes. Cigars made before 2000 will feature a green-coloured seal; on all cigars made after 2000 the seal will be printed in black. The seal should have a unique serial code and a hidden ultraviolet (UV) watermark. Check that the printing is uniformly dense and of good quality.

Next check that the 'Habanos' chevron is in the correct form. On flat-dressed boxes it will appear on the top left corner, while on slide-lid cabinet boxes it will be on the bottom left corner. The chevron should be 2 centimetres (¾ inches) wide

and the word 'Habanos' should be in red outlined in orange-gold. There should be two thick black lines running on the outer edges, and a further two thin gold lines inside. Next to the lettering there should be a silhouette of a tobacco leaf.

Habanos S.A.

Now look at the underneath of the box. Branded into the wood should be the words:

Habanos S.A.
HECHO EN CUBA
Totalmente a mano

Ensure that these words are branded rather than stamped or printed. Also on the bottom there should be a factory/date stamp, which is in code form, comprising letters and numbers.

Distributors' seals

Finally, there should be a seal or stamp indicating where the cigars were distributed. Again, these change quite frequently, so ask the person from whom you're buying the cigars whether he or she can verify that the seal or stamp is genuine. In Britain for example, there should be a brightly coloured Hunters & Frankau 'EMS' (English Market Selection) sticker, while in Canada there should be a Havana House 'duty paid' sticker.

The cigars should be of equal length, the bands should align, be facing upwards, and the printing on the bands should be of high quality. The feet of the cigars should be neatly cut, while the caps too should be smooth and well presented. Look at the ends of the cigars for the 'accordion' fold of truly hand-made cigars, and if any tobacco falls out, don't buy them!

◀ *A worker packs cigars in the traditional cedar boxes at the Partagás factory in Havana, Cuba.*

CIGAR SIZES

There is a bewildering array of cigar sizes and shapes available and, even more confusing, different manufacturers from different parts of the world often call the same sizes and shapes different names. Therefore, although there's no definitive list of cigar sizes, here we'll run through the ones that you're most likely to come across.

When discussing cigar sizes, the word *vitola* will usually crop up. To confuse matters, *vitola* strictly has two meanings – *vitola de galera* and *vitola de salida* (or *fabrica*). Basically, the first is the factory name, which refers to the shape of the cigar; the second is the commercial name of the cigar. Usually the term vitola is used to represent the size and shape of the cigar. Therefore all 'Dalia' vitolas will be 170 millimetres (6¾ inches) long with a ring gauge of 43, whether it's a Ramón Allones 898, a Gloria Cubana Medaille d'Or No. 2 or a Cohíba Siglo V cigar.

Ring gauge

A cigar's diameter is measured in 64ths of an inch; therefore a cigar with a ring gauge of 42 will have a diameter of 42/64ths of an inch, or one with a ring gauge of 32 would have a half-inch diameter. Ring gauges are always measured in fractions of an inch, and in the United States and England, cigars are measured in inches.

Shapes

Cigars are described as either *parejos* (straight edged) or *figurados* (irregular shaped; although this means 'difficult to

Avo Maestro (Parejos)

Santa Damiano Torpedo (Pirámides)

Paul Garmirian Belicoso Fino (Belicoso)

Cuaba Salomon (Perfecto)

COMMON SIZES

Below is a table of the most common sizes of cigars – the 'classic' Havana term and size is followed by a non-Cuban name where different.

Vitola	Length (Variation)	Ring (Variation)
Large Ring Gauge		
*Gran Corona	9¼ in	47
Prominente (Double Corona)	7⅝ in (6¾–7¾)	49 (49–54)
Julieta 2 (Churchill)	7 in (6¾–7⅞)	47 (46–48)
Pirámide (Pyramid)	6⅛ in (6–7)	52 (46–54)
Double Robusto (Toro)	6 in (5⅝–6⅝)	50 (48–54)
Corona Gorda (Grand Corona)	5⅝ in (5⅝–6⅝)	46 (45–47)
Campana (Belicoso)	5½ in (5½–6½)	52 (50–54)
Hermoso No. 4 (Robusto)	5 in (4½–5½)	48 (48–54)
Robusto (Robusto)	4⅞ in (4½–5½)	50 (48–54)
Standard Ring Gauge		
Dalia (Lonsdale)	6¾ in (6½–7¼)	43 (40–44)
Cervante (Lonsdale)	6½ in (6½–7¼)	42 (40–44)
Corona Grande (Long Corona)	6⅛ in (5⅞–6⅜)	42 (40–44)
Corona (Corona)	5½ in (5½–5¾)	42 (40–44)
Nacionales (Corona)	5½ in (5½–5¾)	40 (40–44)
Mareva (Petit Corona)	5 in (4–5)	42 (40–44)
Petit Cetro (Petit Corona)	5 in (4–5)	40 (40–44)
Standard (Petit Corona)	4¾ in (4–5)	40 (40–44)
Franciscano (Petit Corona)	4½ in (4–5)	40 (40–44)
Minuto (Petit Corona)	4⅜ in (4–5)	42 (40–44)
Perla (Petit Corona)	4 in (4–5)	40 (40–44)
Narrow Ring Gauge		
Laguito No.1 (Long Panatela)	7½ in (7–9)	38 (35–39)
Ninfas (Slim Panatela)	7 in (5–7)	33 (30–34)
Laguito No. 2 (Long Panatela)	6 in (7–9)	38 (35–39)
Veguerito (Short Panatela)	5 in (4–5⅜)	37 (35–39)
Belvederas (Short Panatela)	5 in (4–5⅜)	39 (35–39)
Seoane (Short Panatela)	5 in (4–5⅜)	36 (35–39)
Carolina (Short Panatela)	4¾ in (4–5⅜)	36 (35–39)
Cadete (Short Panatela)	4½ in (4–5⅜)	36 (35–39)
Laguito No. 3 (Cigarillos)	4½ in (4–6)	26 (26 or less)
Chicos (Small Panatela)	4⅛ in (4–5)	30 (30–34)
Entreacto	3⅞ in	30

*There also exists a relatively common non-Cuban size known as Giant, which measures 8 in or more with a ring gauge of 50 or more.

roll' and so is sometimes used in reference to the largest *parejos*!). The commonest *figurados* are *pirámides* (wide-gauge end to tapering, pointed cap), *belicoso* (tapering, pointed cap), *perfecto* (both ends pointed) and *culebra* (three slim cigars plaited together). These terms are used differently around the world.

CHOOSING A CIGAR

Now, armed with more information on cigars, how they're made, and the range of shapes and sizes they come in, it's time to start looking for one. The best place to buy cigars is a well-established tobacconist, preferably one with a walk-in humidor, or at least one that stores its cigars in a good-sized humidified cabinet.

◀ *If you want to make sure that you are buying genuine hand-made cigars, check for the words* Totalmente a mano *on the underside of the box.*

Earlier we looked at some of the labels, stamps and stickers found on a genuine box of Havana cigars; let's consider some of the other labels that you might see on boxes of cigars, as this is one good way to avoid mistakenly buying machine-made cigars.

Other labels

On the bottom of the Cuban cigar box the words *Totalmente a mano* are found. This literally means 'Entirely by Hand', and if genuine is a guarantee that the cigars have been rolled in the traditional Cuban way, that is, with long fillers bunched by hand and a wrapper added afterwards, by hand. Also there are the words *Hecho en Cuba* ('Made in Cuba'). Strictly, this only indicates the country of origin and doesn't have any bearing on how the cigars were made. Be wary of any boxes that say *Hecho a mano* (or 'Hand-rolled',

'Hand-finished'). This can mean a variety of things; machine-bunched cigars using inferior, homogenized tobacco as a filler, with their wrappers put on by hand, are often called *Hecho a mano*. To the unwary or uninitiated, these may draw well and taste like 'cigars', but you won't be getting the complex yet subtle flavours that you should get from properly fermented and aged filler. That's okay if you're not paying premium prices, but if you are you're getting a raw deal. Similarly you may come across the phrase *Envuelto a mano* (or 'Hand-packed'). This also means the cigars are machine-made, but that they were selected and packaged by hand.

Size

When you're sure you are looking at a range of premium hand-rolled cigars, the next aspect to consider is the size of the cigar. Generally, cigars with a larger ring gauge will have a more complex or fuller flavour. This is because a greater variety of filler (*ligero, seco* and *volado*) will have been used to make up the gauge. In addition, larger cigars tend to be rolled by more experienced rollers

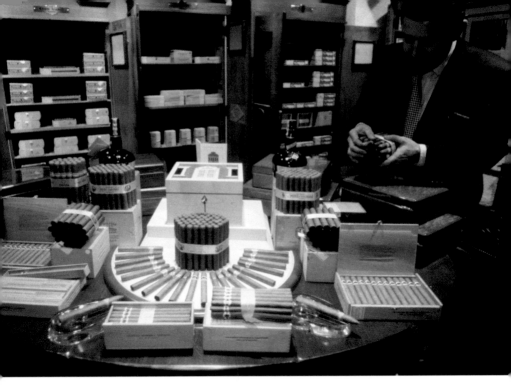

and should therefore have a higher-quality construction. Inexperienced cigar smokers are better off trying a smaller-gauge cigar and working up to the bigger vitolas.

Wrappers

Another important element to consider when choosing cigars is the colour of the wrapper. Although opinion varies about how much flavour the wrapper imparts to the cigar, darker wrappers will tend to have a sweeter, fuller flavour, while paler cigars tend to be milder. But again, flavour does vary according to the blend and age of the filler. Also make sure that the wrapper isn't damaged in any way.

▶ *When choosing a cigar, the colour of the wrapper can be an indication of the cigar's flavour. Generally darker wrappers give a fuller flavour.*

▲ *Tobacconists are there to help you choose a cigar that's right for you so don't be afraid to ask for advice.*

When handling a cigar, be very careful. You only need to gently squeeze a wrapper just below the band to make sure the cigar has the correct springy consistency. If the cigar feels too firm it might be overfilled or plugged; too soft and it may be underfilled; too dry and the wrapper will make a popping, cracking sound; too damp and it will feel spongy.

Finally, don't be afraid to ask about the cigars; if you ask questions you'll more than likely learn something, and most tobacconists are pleased to help out. Find out when the cigars were made. Are they *puros* (meaning the constituent tobacco is all from the same country of origin), or are the wrappers, fillers and binders from different countries? Are the cigars ready to smoke now or should they be aged (see Ageing and Maturing, pages 82–83)? Showing a genuine interest in the cigars and the industry will usually enamour you to a good tobacconist.

LIGHTING UP!

A great deal has been written about how cigars should or shouldn't be smoked; some of it is sensible advice, but much is fanciful. Your character apparently dictates how you hold your cigar, but commonsense might suggest that the size of your hands combined with the size of the cigar would be better defining factors.

One thing that everyone agrees on is that you have to cut the cap off the cigar before you can smoke it; it simply won't draw otherwise. By far the most common tool for this job is the cigar cutter. Cigar cutters come in a vast array of designs, and the body that houses the blade (or blades) can be made of anything from plastic to platinum. As long as the guillotine blade is sharp it should perform the task perfectly adequately. With standard (*parejos*) cigars, look carefully at the cap to see where it is joined to the rest of the cigar; there should be a line running around the cigar. Don't cut beyond this line or you risk watching the wrapper slowly unfurl as you smoke your £15 Upmann. Generally a cut of 2–3 millimetres ($\frac{1}{16}$–$\frac{1}{8}$ inch) should be safe and will allow the cigar to draw sufficiently. With *figuardos* the line of the cap is likely to be further down the cigar's length, so take off about 7–8 millimetres ($\frac{1}{3}$ inch).

Cigar cutters

Alternatives

As well as cigar cutters, there are other cutting devices on the market. Cigar scissors are the preferred tool for many aficionados. Although these are perfectly capable of making clean cuts, they do take some time to get used to, and are not recommended for the novice.

Some people prefer to pierce the cap using a piercer or lance to make a small hole (Winston Churchill was one of these) through which the smoke can flow. Although in theory this device should work satisfactorily, in practice the cigar piercer can compact the filler and create a small wad of tobacco just under the cap. This is then likely to act as a collecting point for tar and oil, which can then ruin the flavour of the smoke as you draw it into your mouth.

Lighting a cigar

Once you've satisfactorily snipped off the cap of the cigar, the next stage is to light it. Do be wary about what you use to light your cigar. At all costs avoid lighters that use liquid fuel. These tend to give off a petrol-like smell, which can easily pervade the cigar when you first draw on it and ruin its flavour for good. Also avoid using matches that have a high sulphur content in the heads, as these can also affect the flavour.

▲ *Although it may appear good-mannered to offer a fellow cigar smoker a light, most prefer to light their own at their own pace.*

The best tools to use for lighting cigars are cigar lighters, which use odourless gas and have a large, adjustable flame, or long, wooden, sulphur-free matches.

To begin lighting the cigar, put the end horizontally in the flame and rotate it slowly, so that it becomes evenly charred. Next put the cigar in your mouth, and holding the flame about 2 centimetres ($^3/_4$ inch) from the end of the cigar, draw slowly while continuing to rotate the cigar. When it appears fully lit, blow on the glowing end to ensure it's burning evenly; if not it will burn faster down one side.

Take your time

Smoking premium cigars should be savoured, and you should only need to take a couple of draws a minute to appreciate fully the complex flavours. Don't panic if the cigar goes out; this isn't a heinous crime, and some cigars are liable to do so. Simply relight it. Nor should you flick the ash off the end of a cigar. The ash helps to keep the cigar burning at the correct temperature. When the ash looks as if it will naturally fall by itself, gently roll the cigar in an ashtray and the ash will come away.

The point at which to extinguish a cigar is entirely up to you. But when the smoke becomes acrid and hot it is a good indicator that you've had the best out of it – and this will usually start to happen about two-thirds of the way down. When you've finished enjoying your cigar don't stub it out, as this will burn the residual oils in the cigar and create an unpleasant smell and an unsightly mess. Simply let the cigar die of its own accord and dispose of it.

Cigar scissors

STORING CIGARS

Cigars can be stored for a surprisingly long time before they have to be smoked – 10 to 15 years is probably about the longest period (depending on the cigar), although some people still derive great pleasure from smoking pre-revolutionary Havanas! But that's probably more for the unique experience rather than for the true flavour of the cigar.

◄ *For most cigar lovers, a humidor is a small investment, which will protect a much larger investment of valuable cigars for many years.*

visits will certainly pay dividends in terms of getting free advice about any cigar-related issues.

Humidors

If, however, you're a more serious smoker (remember the health costs) or you have to travel miles to the nearest tobacconist, then the best option is to invest in a humidor. Like most cigar paraphernalia, humidors come in countless styles and sizes; some can store 25 cigars and will sit neatly on your desk, others can store 2,500 cigars and stand as tall as a fridge-freezer. No matter how much you're prepared to pay, it is essential that the humidor does its job properly. The best humidors are usually made out of mahogany, have well-crafted joints, feel solid and are lined with Spanish cedar; they help maintain the correct level of humidity, slow beetle manifestations and add complementary flavours to your cigars. Humidors usually come fitted with a passive humidifier unit pre-charged with a solution (propylene glycol) that absorbs or releases moisture depending on the humidity in the box, thereby keeping the

To store cigars for any length of time, it's essential that they are kept in an environment with a humidity of 65–70 per cent; if not, the natural oils in the cigar will dry out resulting in a highly unpleasant, bitter-tasting smoke. As the humidity in an average house is around 50 per cent (and even less in air-conditioned homes), you can't keep cigars in a drawer for more than a few days, even if they are in a tube, without running the risk of them drying out.

If you only smoke four or five cigars a week, one option is simply to go to your supplier whenever you run out. All good tobacconists will store their cigars in the correct environment, and your regular

humidity to within 68–72 per cent. When you first buy your humidor, don't put cigars in it straightaway. First make sure that the humidifier unit has been charged with propylene glycol. If so, add distilled water and wait for the humidity to reach the required level. If you're unsure of how much water to add, or whether or not the humidifier has been pre-charged, check with the supplier.

▲ If you choose to buy cigars in a restaurant or bar, make sure they are kept in a humidor, as seen here, so the cigars will be at their best.

very accurate and shouldn't be relied upon. If you're concerned about the humidity level, buy an inexpensive digital hygrometer; these tend to be much more accurate (although they don't look so nice) and many provide a temperature read-out as well.

Hygrometers

A lot of humidors come with built-in dial hygrometers, which provide a humidity reading. Although they look nice, they're not

Temperature

Fortunately cigars like to be kept at a temperature that humans also find comfortable, between 15.5 °C (60 °F) and 21 °C (70 °F), which makes life a bit easier. As long as your humidor is kept in any part of the house that is regularly used and out of direct sunlight, then your cigars should be fine. Obviously, anyone living in areas of climatic extremes needs to be a little more careful about the ambient temperature – particularly if it's often much below 15.5 °C (60 °F) or above 26.5 °C (80 °F) for long periods – as this will eventually affect the temperature in the humidor.

◄ These 60-year-old Cuban cigars in their original humidor will now be dry. However, after six months in a modern humidor, they will be smokable.

AGEING AND MATURING

Ageing cigars is thought by most cigar lovers to be essential if you want to make the most of your premium Dominican, Cuban or Honduran variety. The process will help not only to improve the flavour of the cigar as the different tobaccos used in its construction continue to blend, but it will also improve its performance in terms of how it burns and smokes.

Unfortunately, there are no definitive guidelines as to how long cigars should be aged before they reach their peak. However, there is one thing on which most aficionados agree – most hand-rolled cigars should either be smoked within 10 to 12 weeks of their manufacture or they should not be touched for at least a year. The time between these two dates is often termed the 'period of sickness', and refers to the point during which the cigar starts the maturation process and tastes flat and uninspired. It's somewhat akin to a wine's 'dumb' or 'closed' period. Many wines in their adolescence will show well for a couple of years.

They will then undergo a period when, if opened, they refuse to give up their full and complex bouquet. But after a further period of a few years, they will reach the tertiary stage and spring back to life.

In terms of ageing, cigars and wines do seem to have a lot in common, the so-called 'period of sickness' being one of them. Consider checking with your tobacconist on the date of the cigars you're about to purchase. This may be evident by the factory/date stamp on the bottom of the box, though these stamps are not always that easy to decipher.

▼ *If you don't have a humidor big enough in which to keep your cigars, avoid storing different brands together as the different tobaccos eventually will assume the same personality and characteristics.*

One to two years

Just about all cigars will taste better after ageing for between one and two years, but whereas cigars that are very oily will continue to improve for even longer, milder and lighter cigars, such as those from the Dominican Republic, may well start to become too mellow if left for much longer.

Maturer smokes

Cigars that benefit most from longer periods of ageing, say, three to seven years, tend to be the larger ring, fuller-bodied Cuban or Honduran cigars. These oily creatures, although becoming milder, smoother and less acidic with age, will retain their complex aromas and flavours when their drier counterparts have become bland. However, it's important to watch out for some of the Havanas that undergo long or even additional fermentation, as these are unlikely to mature further.

After ten or so years, it's a bit of a lottery as to how well a cigar will smoke. Some of the fullest-bodied ones may assume a musty aroma, while others take

▲ Some of the best-appointed tobacconists will have walk-in humidors that contain individual 'lockers' in which their customers can keep their own cigars.

on the 'stinky cheese' scent, both of which are highly prized by cigar connoisseurs. Other cigars, however, may by then have lost their flavour altogether.

At any time during the ageing process, if you're feeling a little let down by a much-cherished cigar, there's no danger in letting the rest in the box age for a further year or so and periodically dipping in to see how they're getting on. But this does mean you need to be buying a lot of cigars at any one time, and that always requires a healthy wallet.

Finally, a word of caution: don't try to age a variety of loose cigars together in one small humidor. They will take on the flavours and aromas of their neighbours and eventually they'll all taste the same. It's much better to age cigars in their original boxes or cabinets, and for that you'll need a good-sized humidor, or a friendly tobacconist who'll be happy to store them for you.

CIGAR ETIQUETTE

Pages and pages have been written about 'cigar etiquette', and to be honest it's sometimes difficult to differentiate between 'etiquette' and 'snobbery'. We're only going to touch on the subject here, and restrict advice to either what's commonsense or what to avoid if you don't want to appear foolish.

◀ *These days, if you're smoking a cigar in an enclosed public place in much of Europe or North America you may well be breaking the law.*

if someone asks you to refrain. They may have been unable to find anywhere else to sit but right next to the smoking zone.

Generally, you're an ambassador to the cause, and even if you're in the right, agreeing to move or letting the cigar go out may well be the more politic way forward.

Bands

Bands crop up a lot in cigar etiquette conversations: should you leave them on and should you 'listen' to them? The first is entirely a matter of choice. Some people think that it's bad form to reveal the brand you're smoking and so take the band off; others don't care. If you are going to take the band off, however, light the cigar first and smoke it for a minute or two as this will help to soften the gum on the band, so making it easier to remove without damaging the wrapper.

'Listening to the band' is a reference to rolling a cigar by your ear to hear what sound it makes. In most circles this is a complete no-no. But in fact there is some method to this 'madness'. If the cigar has been kept in conditions too dry for its

I t seems slightly ironic that cigar (and pipe) smokers are often more harshly criticized for their habit than those who puff away on a cigarette – given the love and attention to detail that has gone into a premium hand-rolled cigar compared with a Marlboro or Lucky Strike. But to the uninitiated it's important to remember that cigar smoke 'smells' more than cigarette smoke. Be aware of your surroundings and the people around you. Even if you're in a bona fide designated smoking zone, it's not always right to vociferously assert your rights to smoke

health, the wrapper will crackle and pop as you gently squeeze it, and this may be easier to hear by putting the cigar closer to your ear. But it's probably best to do this in the privacy of your home, behind drawn curtains.

Dipping

A number of people have been known to dip the tip of a cigar into their port, brandy or Cognac before smoking it. This is a bit like digging a big hole in a Christmas Stilton cheese and filling it with port. It ruins the flavour of the cheese and makes a horrid mess; and so with the dipped cigar. If you must, go ahead, but you'll get some strange looks.

Cutting and lighting

Don't cut the end off someone's cigar without at least asking that person first. Most people much prefer to do this themselves, and just think how you'd look if you took off too much. Similarly, don't hold a lighter or match up for someone to light a cigar. It can force them to light the cigar too hastily and ruin it. Much better to let people go at their own pace and hand them the lighter or box of matches.

Ash

Finally, be aware of your ash. A number of cigar smokers swear that ash does wonders for a carpet, but this attitude is guaranteed to give even considerate smokers a bad name. Use an ashtray.

◄ *Although you may think you're being considerate, snipping the end off a cigar is best left to the cigar's owner, particularly if it's a rare Cohiba.*

3

The Cigar Directory provides a listing of established cigar brands from Cuba, the Dominican Republic and other cigar-producing countries from around the world, and is ordered alphabetically by cigar brand. Some of the cigars are only available in the United States, while others, primarily those from Cuba, are not available in the United States due to the US embargo on Cuban products.

The Cigar Directory also tells the history behind some of the world's most famous brands – such as Cohíba, H. Upmann, Punch and CAO; how the cigars came to be made; the fascinating stories of the people behind them; and the country of origin of the tobacco used in the cigars. The Cigar Directory deliberately does not give subjective opinions on the flavour of the cigars, but does indicate their strengths.

In general, we would recommend that those new to cigars begin with brands that are considered mild, such as some of those from the Dominican Republic, and slowly work up to the stronger, full-bodied examples, many of which come from Cuba. These are often an acquired taste and only experienced cigar aficionados will fully appreciate their complex, rich flavours and aromas, and their more robust strengths.

KEY TO SYMBOLS

- Hand-made
- Strength
- Country of origin of the filler
- Country of origin of the binder
- Country of origin of the wrapper

CIGAR DIRECTORY

ARTURO FUENTE [DOMINICAN REPUBLIC]

Despite numerous setbacks in its long history spanning four generations, the Fuente family is today producing some of the most sought-after cigars in America and the rest of the world. As with so many of the most famous cigar-producing families, the Fuente family's cigar roots are based in Cuba where Arturo Fuente learned how to cultivate tobacco and manufacture hand-made cigars from his father. The company is now based in the Dominican Republic.

In 1912 Arturo Fuente founded a small cigar factory at the back of the family's home in Ybor City, Tampa, Florida, and it was here that Arturo's son, Carlos Sr, the present chairman of the company, discovered his passion for cigars. After acquiring the business from his father, Carlos Sr made unsuccessful attempts to establish factories first in Nicaragua and then in Honduras following the demise of cigar manufacturing in Florida. Both fledgling factories were destroyed by fire. Undeterred, Carlos Sr and his son Carlos Jr, who is now president of Arturo Fuente, moved to the Dominican Republic in 1980, where they established a small operation employing just seven workers.

FUENTE FUENTE (OPUSX)
⬚ Ⓢ Full-bodied ◉ Dominican Rep ◉ Dominican Rep
◎ Dominican Rep

Name	Length/Inches	Ring Gauge	Shape
Belicoso XXX	4⅝	49	Figurado
Fuente Fuente	5⅝	46	Coronas
Petit Lancero	6¼	38	Panatelas
Double Corona	7⅝	49	Double Corona
Perfecxion A	9⅝	47	Giants

ARTURO FUENTE (GRAN RESERVA)
⬚ Ⓢ Medium to Full-bodied ◉ Dominican Rep
◉ Dominican Rep ◎ Cameroon/Connecticut/Ecuador

Name	Length/Inches	Ring Gauge	Shape
Exquisito	4½	33	Demi-tasse
Brevas Royal	5½	42	Coronas
Double Château Fuente			
Maduro	6¾	50	Churchill
Sun Grown	6¾	50	Churchill
Presidente	6½	50	Toro
Canones	8½	52	Double Corona

OpusX Petit Lancero

The family's innovative yet uncompromising approach to the production of hand-made cigars soon generated an ever-growing band of loyal customers in the United States, and was rewarded in the autumn of 1994 when a cigar wrapped with shade leaf from their own farm, Château de la Fuente, beat several Havanas in a *Cigar Aficionado* magazine tasting. Sceptics had seriously doubted the wisdom of a Dominican-grown wrapper; historically, cigars from the Republic used wrappers grown in Cameroon or the United States. The now-famous Fuente Fuente OpusX is a highly favoured cigar by connoisseurs around the world, but the extremely long ageing process, on which Carlos Fuente Sr and Jr refuse to compromise, has resulted in a long backlist of orders. However, the future looks promising for fans of this illustrious cigar, as the family is currently preparing an additional 60 hectares (150 acres) of land near their present farm, which they believe will be as good as, if not better than, the soil of Château de la Fuente for growing wrapper leaves.

As well as the OpusX range, Arturo Fuente also produce their famous Gran Reserva cigars, which use Cameroon, Connecticut Shade and more recently Ecuadorian Sun Grown wrappers around quality vintage tobaccos. The consistently well-rolled cigars are then aged in Spanish cedar vaults.

Other popular ranges from the Château de la Fuente include the Don Carlos – 'Pride of the Fuente Family' – and the Hemingway, responsible for bringing back the lost *Perfecto* and the Añejo series.

OpusX Double Corona

ARTURO FUENTE (DON CARLOS)
Medium to Full-bodied ● Dominican Rep ● Dominican Rep ● Cameroon

Name	Length/Inches	Ring Gauge	Shape
Belicosos	5⅜	52	Figurado
Double Robusto	5¾	52	Toro
Don Carlos No. 2	6	55	Torpedo
Presidente	6½	50	Toro

ARTURO FUENTE (HEMINGWAY)
Medium to Full-bodied ● Dominican Rep ● Dominican Rep ● Cameroon

Name	Length/Inches	Ring Gauge	Shape
Best Seller	5	55	Figurado
Classic	7	48	Figurado
Masterpiece	9¼	52	Giants

AVO [DOMINICAN REPUBLIC]

Avo Uvezian, the gifted pianist and composer from whom this increasingly popular Dominican brand gets its name, was born in Beirut in 1926. His mother was an accomplished singer, and his father a composer and symphony orchestra conductor. Avo's first musical love was jazz, and he achieved notable success in the Middle East as a teenager in his band The Lebanon Boys.

Avo moved to the United States in 1947, where he was accepted into the prestigious Juilliard School of Music, studying classical piano and composition. Following a brief spell in the army, Avo fulfilled his desire to become a successful musician, playing with most of the jazz greats during the 1950s and 1960s.

The Avo brand

Avo's move to Puerto Rico in the early 1980s was the catalyst for his next passion – cigars. His love for cigars resulted in him developing his own unique blend, which he would give away to customers in his restaurant and piano bar. The popularity of his cigars spurred him on to develop the AVO brand, with the help of the cigar manufacturer and connoisseur Hendrik Kelner, who was based in the Dominican Republic.

By 1988 the first AVO cigars became available in the United States, and their early success resulted in Davidoff paying an estimated $10 million for the exclusive distribution rights in 1995.

Today AVO produce around three million cigars each year from their factory based in the Cibao Valley, the tobacco heartland of the Dominican Republic. The range of cigars includes the XO Trio, XO Quartetto, Domaine, Signature, Classic and Limited series, including the AVO Legacy, AVO 77 (released as a celebration of Avo's 77th birthday), AVO 22 (comprising simply of two perfectos), the AVO Limited Edition '2005', AVO 80th Anniversary (released in 2006 to celebrate Avo's 80th birthday) and most recently the AVO LE 07. Apart from the latter, most of the Limited Edition cigars are increasingly hard to find. All AVO cigars have a reputation for being consistently well made, and this is reflected in the price – these are not the cheapest cigars around.

Although using mostly Dominican fillers and binders and Connecticut Shade wrappers, many AVO branded cigars are surprisingly robust and flavoursome.

XO Trio Maestoso

AVO (XO TRIO)

📄 💲 Mild to Medium ◉ Dominican Rep ◎ Dominican Rep
◑ Connecticut Shade

Name	Length/Inches	Ring Gauge	Shape
Intermezzo	5½	50	Robusto
Preludio	6	40	Lonsdale
Maestoso	7	48	Churchill

AVO (XO QUARTETTO)

📄 💲 Mild to Medium ◉ Dominican Rep ◎ Dominican Rep
◑ Connecticut Shade

Name	Length/Inches	Ring Gauge	Shape
Allegro	4½	34	Petit Panatella
Presto	5	31	Small Panatella
Notturno	5	42	Petit Corona
Serenata	5¾	38	Panatella

AVO (DOMAINE)

📄 💲 Mild to Medium ◉ Dominican Rep ◎ Dominican Rep
◑ Ecuador

Name	Length/Inches	Ring Gauge	Shape
Domaine 20	4⅗	52	Perfecto
Domaine 10	5	50	Robusto
Domaine 60	5	43	Corona
Domaine 40	6	52	Figurado
Domaine 50	6	54	Perfecto
Domaine 30	6¾	48	Churchill

AVO (MADURO)

📄 💲 Mild to Medium ◉ Dominican Rep ◎ Dominican Rep
◑ Connecticut Broadleaf

Name	Length/Inches	Ring Gauge	Shape
Belicoso	6	50	Belicoso
No. 2	6	50	Toro
Pirámide	7	36/54	Figurado
No. 3	7½	52	Double Corona

AVO (80TH ANNIVERSARY)

📄 💲 Mild to Medium ◉ Dominican Rep ◎ Dominican Rep
◑ Ecuador

Name	Length/Inches	Ring Gauge	Shape
80th Anniversary	6	52	Belicoso

XO Quartetto Serenata

AVO [CONTINUED]

1 XO Quartetto Presto   **2** XO Notturno (Tubo) **3** XO Trio Preludio

4 Domaine 40   **5** Domaine 10

BOLIVAR [CUBA/DOMINICAN REPUBLIC]

T he early history of this most enduring of Cuban brands is veiled in mist, but it is believed that it was founded in Europe, most likely England, in 1901 by the Rocha company, becoming registered as a Cuban brand in 1921.

The brand is named after the famous nineteenth-century Venezuelan revolutionary Simón Bolívar, who liberated much of South America from Spanish rule during a number of campaigns between 1813 and 1825; and it is the portrait of 'El Liberator' that adorns the bands and boxes of the cigars today.

The Bolívar company was once famous for making the smallest vitola ever produced. Known as the Delgado, it measured 4.76 centimetres (1⅞ inches) and had a ring gauge of 20. The company's reputation for creating small cigars reached a pinnacle when it produced a miniature box of cigars to be placed in a doll's house in the royal nursery at Windsor Castle.

Following José Rocha's death in 1954, the Bolívar brand, along with another, 'La Gloria Cubana', was bought by the Cifuentes family, then owners of the Partagás factory – the second-largest tobacco factory at that time. Following the Cuban Revolution the Cifuentes family fled Cuba, and Bolívar passed into the hands of the state-run Cubatabaco.

Ageing qualities

Prized for being among the fullest-bodied of all Cuban brands, Bolívar cigars are not for the inexperienced smoker. However, having the reputation for being one of the least expensive of Cuban premium

BOLIVAR (DOMINICAN)

📖 💲 Medium to Full 🔘 Dominican Rep/Nicaragua 🔘 Connecticut Broadleaf 🔘 Honduras

Name	Length/Inches	Ring Gauge	Shape
Robusto	5½	50	Robusto
Toro	6	52	Toro
Lonsdale	6½	45	Londsdale
Churchill	7	49	Julieta

Cuban Inmensas

cigars (although they are almost on a par with most other Havanas today), they are a firm favourite of cigar connoisseurs around the world, particularly in Britain and Germany. Known for their full and rich taste, Bolívar cigars are also prized by aficionados for their superb ageing qualities, which are due to the abundant oils in the tobacco used in their construction. For this reason well-aged Bolívars are extremely sought after on the vintage market – the Bolívar Cigar Gold Medal, which was officially discontinued in the late 1980s, being one of the most desirable collector's items. Although a German tobacconist in Cologne, La Casa del Habano had a limited edition of this most celebrated of cigars made in 2005 – but with only 1,000 boxes of 10 made, they're unlikely to be widely available.

For newcomers to this illustrious brand, the Petit Coronas are recommended, being slightly milder than the other cigars in the series.

There are a number of machine-made Bolívar cigars available, which also age surprisingly well, but do be wary if you think you've picked up a bargain hand-made Havana.

Dominican Bolívar

The Dominican brand was established by Ramón Cifuentes, following the family's departure from Cuba, and today the brand, along with Dominican Partagás, is owned by General Cigar Dominicana. Although initially much milder than their Cuban counterparts, in more recent years Dominican Bolívars have become increasingly robust, in part due to the use of Honduran ligero wrappers.

BOLIVAR (CUBAN)
📄 💲 Full-bodied 🔘 Cuba ▨ Cuba 🌑 Cuba

Name	Length/Inches	Ring Gauge	Shape
Royal Corona	4⅘	50	Robusto
Bonitas	5	40	Petit Cetro
Petit Corona	5	42	Mareva
Corona	5½	42	Corona
Corona Extra	5½	44	Corona Gorda
Belicosos Finos	5½	52	Figurados
Lonsdales	6½	42	Cervantes
Inmensas	6¾	43	Dalia
Corona Gigantes	7	47	Julieta
Churchill	7	47	Julieta

1 Cuban Corona **2** Cuban Lonsdales
3 Cuban Belicosos Finos **4** Cuban Royal Corona

CAO [NICARAGUA/HONDURAS]

Criollo Pampas

After an initially shaky start in the cigar world, CAO has grown to be one of the most innovative and successful US-owned cigar companies. CAO wasn't actually founded to produce cigars. Cano A. Ozgener, a former engineer at DuPont, Nashville, began the company to manufacture pipes. Cano, a confirmed pipe smoker, used his engineering skills to improve the performance of his beloved meerschaum pipes, and soon local tobacconists were sufficiently impressed that Cano decided to leave DuPont to set up his new venture in 1977. After a brief foray into the cigar business in 1980, which was not a success, Ozgener reverted to producing pipes, while also developing a range of humidors, many of which featured his own unique humidification system.

In 1995, realizing that pipes and humidors were not going to expand his business as rapidly as he wanted, Ozgener once again moved into selling cigars, with a brand simply called CAO. They were made at the Honduran Fabrica de Tabacos Oriente factory by Nestor Plasencia. Featuring filler from Nicaragua and Mexico, Honduran binders and Connecticut Shade wrappers, the cigars were well received, but as with many companies during this boom period, consistency was a problem.

But by the late 1990s and into the new millennium CAO grew in popularity, largely thanks to the success of an extremely popular

CAO (CAMEROON)
Medium ◉ Nicaragua ⊘ Nicaragua ◖ Cameroon

Name	Length/Inches	Ring Gauge	Shape
Robusto	5	50	Robusto
Corona	5½	45	Corona
No. 1	5½	46	Figurado
Belicoso	6	54	Belicoso
Churchill	7	48	Churchill

CAO (BRAZILIA)
Medium ◉ Nicaragua ⊘ Nicaragua ◖ Brazil

Name	Length/Inches	Ring Gauge	Shape
Piranha	4½	46	Corona Gorda
Gold	5	56	Robusto
Amazon	6	60	Toro
Samba	6¼	54	Figurado
Ipanema	7	50	Churchill
Anaconda	8	58	Figurado

maduro brand, hard-hitting, eye-catching advertising, and the policy of regularly bringing out new brands. Many of these have been subsequently very well received, particularly in the United States, and their success prompted CAO to purchase two of their own factories in 2003, one in Danlí, Honduras, the other near Estelí in Nicaragua.

CAO's latest brand, Vision, is the most daring to date. The cigar is the first CAO offering to feature a Dominican binder and wrapper, with a blended filler from Nicaragua, Brazil and the Dominican Republic. But even more eye-catching is the box in which the cigars ship. It has a digital hygrometer on the outside, a humidifier pack on the inside and blue neon lights that light up when the lid is opened. The lights are powered by six replaceable AA batteries, and replacement humidifier packs are available when the initial pack runs out. The idea is that the box will double up as a travel humidor.

Brazilia Piranha

CAO (MADURO)

Medium to Full-bodied Nicaragua/Dominican Rep
Ecuador Connecticut Broadleaf

Name	Length/Inches	Ring Gauge	Shape
Rothschild	4½	50	Rothschild
Robusto	5	50	Robusto
Corona	5½	42	Corona
Toro	5½	55	Toro
Belicoso	6	54	Belicoso
Churchill	7⅞	48	Churchill

CAO (CRIOLLO)

Medium to Full-bodied Nicaragua Nicaragua
Nicaragua

Name	Length/Inches	Ring Gauge	Shape
Pampas	4	38	Short Panatela
Pato	4⅞	50	Robusto
Mancha	5⅝	46	Corona Gorda
Bomba	6	50	Toro
Conquistador	6⅛	52	Figurado

CAO (VISION)

Medium Dominican Rep/Nicaragua/Brazil
Dominican Rep Dominican Rep

Name	Length/Inches	Ring Gauge	Shape
Catalyst	5	50	Robusto
Epiphany	6	50	Toro
Prana	6¼	52	Figurado

CAO [CONTINUED]

1 Criollo Pato

2 Cameroon No. 1   **3** Maduro Robusto

COHIBA [CUBA]

Despite being a relatively new Cuban brand (it was founded in 1968), Cohíba cigars are today widely accepted as being among the finest in the world – but with a price tag to match.

The history of Cohíba cigars –the word is thought to be the Taino Indian word for 'cigar' – is a fascinating one, and despite its young age, the brand has already passed into Cuban folklore. The story goes that during the mid-1960s one of Fidel Castro's bodyguards regularly enjoyed a supply of cigars made for him by a local cigar roller, Eduardo Rivera. Castro became so enamoured with the blend of Rivera's cigars that he brought Rivera to Havana and set him to work rolling his cigars in the suburb of El Laguito in a building of the same name, which was being used as a school to train *torcedores* and *torcedoras* (male and female cigar rollers).

In 1968, under the guidance of the master *torcedor* Avelino Lara, who took over from Rivera in the same year, it was decided that the cigars should be produced – albeit in small quantities – for use as gifts in diplomatic and government circles; and so the first three vitolas went into production – the Lancero, the Corona Especiale and the Panatela – all unique sizes and all, of course, favourites of Castro.

Linea 1492

For the next 14 years, only foreign heads of state, their advisors and high-ranking Cuban government officials had the pleasure of enjoying the world's finest cigars, until 1982 when Castro and Cubatabaco decided it was time to make the brand available to the rest of the world. In 1989 three more sizes were added – the Esplendido, the Robusto and the uniquely sized Exquisito. Then, to mark the 500th anniversary of Columbus' discovery of Cuba, the Siglo (meaning 'century') series of five cigars (known as the Linea 1492) was introduced in 1992, with an additional Siglo VI added in 2003. Other limited edition releases include the Pirámide (2001), the Double Corona (2003), the Sublime (2004) and another Pirámide (2006).

Once manufactured solely at the prestigious El Laguito factory, the increasing number of vitolas available has meant that some are rolled at other factories, including the José Martí (formerly H. Upmann) and Francisco Perez German (formerly Partagás) factories. The cigars are revered for the quality of the tobacco – the factories making them having their pick of the finest tobacco grown on Cuba – and their fine construction – only the best rollers make Cohíba cigars.

Linea Clasica

Esplendido

Red Dot Corona

Red Dot

Cigars bearing the brand 'Cohíba' and manufactured in the Dominican Republic have been sold in the United States since the early 1980s by General Cigar Company, who astutely registered the name in the United States in the late 1970s. This brand was further revised in 1997, and is now known as 'Red Dot' Cohíba, due to the 'o' being filled with red ink. There are ten vitolas in the 'Red Dot' series, all with Cameroon wrappers, binders from Indonesia and blended filler from the Dominican Republic.

COHIBA (LINEA CLASICA)
📄 Ⓢ Medium to Full-bodied ◉ Cuba ◉ Cuba ◯ Cuba

Name	Length/Inches	Ring Gauge	Shape
Panatela	4½	26	Panatela
Robusto	4⅞	50	Robusto
Exquisito	5	36	Seoane
Corona Especial	6	38	Laguito No. 2
Esplendido	7	47	Julieta
Lancero	7½	38	Laguito No. 1

COHIBA (MADURO)
📄 Ⓢ Medium to Full-bodied ◉ Cuba ◉ Cuba ◯ Cuba

Name	Length/Inches	Ring Gauge	Shape
Secretos	4⅜	40	Reyes
Magicos	4½	52	Robusto
Genios	5½	52	Robusto

COHIBA (LINEA 1492)
📄 Ⓢ Medium to Full-bodied ◉ Cuba ◉ Cuba ◯ Cuba

Name	Length/Inches	Ring Gauge	Shape
Siglo I	4	26	Perla
Siglo II	5	42	Mareva
Siglo IV	5⅝	44	Corona Gorda
Siglo VI	5⅞	52	Canonanzo
Siglo III	6⅛	42	Corona Grande
Siglo V	6¾	52	Dalia

COHIBA (LIMITED EDITIONS)
📄 Ⓢ Medium to Full-bodied ◉ Cuba ◉ Cuba ◯ Cuba

Name	Length/Inches	Ring Gauge	Shape
Pirámide	6³⁄₁₀	52	Pirámide
Sublime 2004	6½	54	Sublime
Double Corona	7³⁄₅	49	Prominente

1 Limited Editions Pirámíde **2** Limited Editions Sublime 2004

3 Linea 1492 Siglo VI (Tubo) **4** Linea Clasica Panatela **5** Linea 1492 Siglo I

CUABA [CUBA]

Divinos

C uaba is the most recent of all the brands to come out of Cuba. The name is taken from the Taino Indian word for a particular type of bush that grows abundantly all over the island, and which, because it's highly flammable, was thought to be used during the ancient Indians' religious ceremonies to light the cigars that played a fundamental role in their religious practices.

The brand's well-publicized launch took place in the autumn of 1996 in London's famous Claridge's Hotel – and for a good reason. All the cigars in the Cuaba range are figurados (perfectos), a shape that was particularly favoured in England during the nineteenth century but that during most of the twentieth century was largely forgotten. It was the intention of Carlos González, the man responsible for developing the brand, to reignite some interest in this forgotten vitola – and the general opinion is that he has succeeded very well.

Flying torcedores

During the launch some 15 *torcedores* were flown over from Cuba to England to demonstrate the skilled art of rolling such difficult cigars. The earliest examples of Cuaba cigars, formed without the help of moulds, were noticeably inconsistent in their shape, and these are now highly collectible – the Romeo y Julieta factory (now called the Briones Montoto) where the cigars are made has resolved the issue by resorting to perfecto-shaped moulds to ensure the cigars are more consistent.

CUABA
📄 🌑 Medium to Full-bodied ◉ Cuba ◕ Cuba ◯ Cuba

Name	Length/Inches	Ring Gauge	Shape
Divinos	4	43	Perfecto
Tradicionales	4¾	42	Perfecto
Generosos	5¼	42	Perfecto
Exclusivos	5⅝	46	Perfecto
Distinguidos	6³⁄₁₀	52	Perfecto
Salomones	7⅕	57	Perfecto
Diademas	9⅕	55	Perfecto

1 Diademas **2** Salomones **3** Exclusivos

CUESTA-REY [DOMINICAN REPUBLIC]

Centro Fino Sun Grown
Pyramid No. 9

The Cuesta-Rey brand – once the largest cigar-manufacturing city in the world – was founded in Tampa, Florida by a young Spanish immigrant, Angel La Madrid Cuesta, in 1884. Soon after, Cuesta went into partnership with Peregrino Rey, and their factory quickly earned a reputation for making excellent hand-made 'clear Havanas', which were cigars made entirely from imported Cuban tobacco.

Cuesta-Rey was acquired by M&N Cigar Manufacturers Inc. in 1958, which in turn became the J.C. Newman Cigar Co., the oldest family-owned premium cigar manufacturer in the United States, and one of the few cigar companies left in Ybor City, Tampa. Also in 1958 the celebrated Cuesta-Rey Cabinet Selection was born with the Cuesta-Rey No. 95, the first hand-made cigar to utilize a Cameroon wrapper. The popularity of the No. 95 resulted in the rapid addition of three more vitolas, the No. 898, No. 1 and No. 2. These four cigars made up the Cuesta-Rey Cabinet Selection until the 1980s, when J.C. Newman joined forces with the famous Fuente family to form the Fuente & Newman Cigar Family and the Cuesta-Rey factory was moved to the Dominican Republic. This union saw the addition of the No. 1884 – the first Cabinet Selection cigar to be rolled with Connecticut Shade wrapper. In 1999 the No. 47 was added to the range, using a blend created by Carlos Fuente Sr and available with either a Cameroon or Connecticut Broadleaf maduro wrapper.

CUESTA-REY (CENTRO FINO SUN GROWN)

📄 🚬 Medium to Full-bodied ⬤ Dominican Rep ◉ Dominican Rep
◐ Ecuador

Name	Length/Inches	Ring Gauge	Shape
Robusto No. 7	4½	54	Robusto
Belicoso No. 11	4⅘	50	Belicoso
No. 60	6	50	Toro
Pyramid No. 9	6⅕	52	Figurado
Captiva	6¼	42	Lonsdale
Churchill No 1	7	49	Churchill

As well as the Cabinet Selection, Cuesta-Rey also produce the Centenario Collection, a series of cigars that are available with either a smooth, creamy Connecticut Shade or slightly fuller Broadleaf wrapper, and for the more adventurous the much punchier Ecuadorian Centro Fino Sun Grown maduro wrapper cigars, which were introduced in 2003 in response to consumer demand for fuller-bodied cigars. These feature Sumatra-seed wrappers grown in the fertile Quevedo region of Ecuador wrapped around a blend of five-year-old ligero Dominican filler, and have successfully turned cigar lovers used to more powerful sticks onto the brand.

All Cuesta-Rey cigars have a reputation for good consistent construction and the presentation, notably the decorative bands and boxes, has won plaudits from around the world.

Centenario Robusto
No. 7

CUESTA-REY (CABINET)
📄 🚬 Mild to Medium ⚫ Dominican Rep ⚫ Dominican Rep
⬭ Connecticut Shade

Name	Length/Inches	Ring Gauge	Shape
No. 47	4¾	47	Robusto
No. 95	6½	42	Lonsdale
(Cameroon wrapper)			
No. 1884	6¾	44	Lonsdale
No. 2	7	36	Panatela
No. 898	7	49	Julieta
No. 1	8½	52	Presidente

CUESTA-REY (CENTENARIO)
📄 🚬 Mild to Medium ⚫ Dominican Rep ⚫ Dominican Rep
⬭ Connecticut Shade/Connecticut Broadleaf

Name	Length/Inches	Ring Gauge	Shape
Robusto No. 7	4½	50	Robusto
Belicoso No. 11	4⅞	50	Figurado
No. 5	5½	43	Corona
Milano	5½	48	Robusto
No. 60	6	50	Toro
Pyramid No. 9	6¼	52	Figurado
Rivera	7	34	Long Panatela
Aristocrat	7¼	48	Churchill

DAVIDOFF [DOMINICAN REPUBLIC]

Mille 2000

Founded by one of the most respected figures in the cigar world, Zino Davidoff, the brand Davidoff, like the man, remains the epitome of style and good taste. Zino's family opened a tobacco store in Geneva, Switzerland, in 1912, and while working for the shop Zino travelled throughout much of Central and South America during the 1920s sourcing some of the finest cigars, culminating in a two-year period working on a tobacco farm in Cuba.

Châteaux

Zino returned to Geneva in 1930 and proceeded to expand the cigar side of the family business, where his greatest success was in developing and marketing the Hoyo de Monterrey Châteaux selection of cigars, each of which was named after a celebrated wine-making region of France.

In an unprecedented move, in 1967 Cubatabaco, the state-run Cuban tobacco manufacturer established shortly after the Revolution, approached Zino with a view to developing his own brand of cigars for sale in his upmarket stores. This acknowledgement of Zino's experience and expertise was reinforced when it was decided that the Davidoff brand of cigars was to be produced in the prestigious El Laguito factory, home of Castro's beloved Cohíba cigars.

Two years later, in 1969, the first Cuban Davidoffs were released onto the global market. The No. 1, No. 2 and Ambassadrice were created in the same vitola as the first Cohíbas (Laguito No. 1, No. 2 and No. 3), further evidence of the honour that was bestowed upon the Davidoff brand. Also produced were the now-famous Châteaux series of cigars, which were newly created specifically for Davidoff from the Hoyo de Monterrey brand. Included in this series were the Haut-Brion, Lafite, Lafite-Rothschild, Latour, Margaux, Mouton Rothschild and Yquem cigars.

Mille

These highly successful cigars were followed during the 1970s by another series known as the Mille (Thousand), which included the 1000, 2000, 3000, 4000 and 5000 series. These were not as full-bodied as the Châteaux range, but were not as mild as the No. 1, No. 2, Ambassadrice and the Dom Pérignon, the last being created at the same time as the Mille series. Finally, in 1986 to celebrate Zino's 80th birthday, the limited edition 80 Aniversario was released.

Then in 1990, following a number of disputes over the quality of the cigars and allegedly over the ownership of the brand, Zino reluctantly terminated the partnership with Cubatabaco, left his beloved Cuba and began producing cigars under the Davidoff brand in the Dominican Republic alongside Hendrik Kelner. Dominican Davidoffs, although using the same vitolas as their Cuban counterparts, do not deliberately try to emulate the Cuban cigars; it seems likely that Davidoff and Kelner appreciated that the milder Dominican tobacco would need an entirely new approach. Although the new Davidoffs didn't necessarily appeal to those who preferred the stronger, more complex Cuban cigars, their consistently high manufacturing qualities have won them plaudits from around the world.

DAVIDOFF (ANIVERSARIO)
Medium to Full-bodied Dominican Rep Dominican Rep Connecticut Shade

Name	Length/Inches	Ring Gauge	Shape
No. 3	6	50	Toro
No. 2	7	48	Churchill
No. 1	8²/₃	48	Gran Corona

DAVIDOFF (CLASSIC)
Mild to Medium Dominican Rep Dominican Rep Connecticut Shade

Name	Length/Inches	Ring Gauge	Shape
Ambassadrice	4⅝	26	Carolinas
No. 3	5⅛	30	Laguito No. 3
No. 2	6	38	Laguito No. 2
No. 3	7½	38	Laguito No. 1

Classic Ambassadrice

DAVIDOFF (MILLE)
Mild to Medium Dominican Rep Dominican Rep Connecticut Shade

Name	Length/Inches	Ring Gauge	Shape
1000	4⅝	34	Panatela
2000	5	43	Mareva
3000	7	33	Ninfa
4000	6³/₃₂	42	Corona Grande
5000	5⅝	46	Corona Gorda

Zino Davidoff died in 1994, but the brand has continued to develop and now features six series, including the Classic, Aniversario, Mille, Millennium (which uses a fuller-bodied Cuban-seed wrapper from Ecuador), Grand Cru (considered the most complex in the range), and Special (all of which feature a hefty 50 ring gauge).

As you'd expect from the Davidoff brand, the cigars are extremely well made and presented in a classic, understated yet elegant white band.

DAVIDOFF (MILLENNIUM)
📖 🌑 Mild to Medium ◉ Dominican Rep ◍ Dominican Rep
◐ Ecuador

Name	Length/Inches	Ring Gauge	Shape
Petit Corona	4½	41	Petit Corona
Robusto	5¼	50	Robusto
Lonsdale	6	43	Lonsdale
Pirámide	6⅛	52	Figurado
Churchill	6¾	48	Churchill

DAVIDOFF (GRAND CRU)
📖 🌑 Mild to Medium ◉ Dominican Rep ◍ Dominican Rep
◐ Connecticut Shade

Name	Length/Inches	Ring Gauge	Shape
No. 5	4	40	Petit Corona
No. 4	4⅝	40	Corona
No. 3	5	42	Corona
No. 2	5⅝	42	Corona
No. 1	6³⁄₃₂	42	Lonsdale

DAVIDOFF (SPECIAL)
📖 🌑 Mild to Medium ◉ Dominican Rep ◍ Dominican Rep
◐ Connecticut Shade

Name	Length/Inches	Ring Gauge	Shape
Special R	4⅞	50	Robusto
Short Perfecto	5	50	Perfecto
Special T	6	50	Figurado
Double R	7½	50	Churchill

1 Aniversario No. 1 **2** Millennium Pirámide **3** Classic No. 2 **4** Special R (Tubo)

DON DIEGO [DOMINICAN REPUBLIC]

Established in 1964 on the Canary Islands, the brand moved to the Dominican Republic in 1982. The use of filler and binder tobacco from the Dominican Republic and Connecticut Shade wrappers, as used in the Playboy series (commissioned by *Playboy* magazine), ensured that Don Diego cigars received a warm reception in the United States during the boom years, when fashion was for a milder cigar. More recently Don Diego cigars have become fuller bodied. The Aniversario range, for example, uses Sumatran-seed Ecuadorian wrappers, a rich Connecticut Broadleaf binder, and a blend of Dominican, Peruvian and Nicaraguan filler, creating an oily, robust cigar.

DON DIEGO

Mild to Medium ◉ Dominican Rep/Brazil ◉ Dominican Rep ◯ Connecticut Shade

Name	Length/Inches	Ring Gauge	Shape
Babies	4³/₄	33	Seaone
Corona	5½	42	Corona
Grande Natural	6	50	Toro
Royal Palm	6¹/₈	36	Panatela
Lonsdale	6⁵/₈	42	Lonsdale
Churchill	7	54	Corona

DON DIEGO (PLAYBOY)

Mild to Medium ◉ Dominican Rep ◉ Dominican Rep ◯ Connecticut Shade

Name	Length/Inches	Ring Gauge	Shape
Robusto	5	50	Robusto
Lonsdale	6½	42	Lonsdale
Gran Corona	6³/₄	48	Gran Corona
Churchill	7³/₄	50	Julieta

DON DIEGO (ANIVERSARIO)

Medium ◉ Dominican Rep/Nicaragua/Peru ◉ Connecticut Broadleaf ◯ Ecuador

Name	Length/Inches	Ring Gauge	Shape
Lord Rothchilde	5	52	Robusto
No. 3	5¹/₂	44	Robusto
Toro	6	54	Toro
No. 3 (Belicoso)	6¹/₈	52	Belicoso
Lonsdale	6¹/₂	42	Lonsdale
Prime Minister	7	54	Presidente

Don Diego Churchill

1 Playboy Robusto **2** Lonsdale **3** Corona

DUNHILL [DOMINICAN REPUBLIC]

SINCE 1907

Alfred Dunhill opened his first tobacco store in 1907 to distribute and sell Cuban cigars. Dunhill were the tobacconist of choice for the rich and famous, including George VI and Winston Churchill, selling premium-brand cigars such as Montecristo and Romeo y Julieta. In 1935, the first 'house' brand appeared under the name Don Cándido, which was created exclusively for Dunhill by the master Cuban blender Cándido Vega Díaz. This brand was followed by another exclusive house brand, the Don Alfredo range, which was produced in the H. Upmann factory from around 1963 onwards.

In 1982 Cubatabaco and Dunhill went into partnership to produce a series of cigars with the famous Dunhill branding. Although the cigars were well-received and are highly sought after, the relationship between Dunhill and Cubatabaco wasn't to last and production of Dunhill cigars ceased in 1991.

Today the Dunhill cigar brand is licensed to BAT (British American Tobacco) who produce two ranges of cigars, both of which are produced in the Dominican Republic. The mild Dunhill Aged series features Dominican and Brazilian filler and Connecticut wrappers, while the more robust Signed series uses an Ecuadorian wrapper, a US Broadleaf binder, and filler from the Dominican Republic and Colombia.

DUNHILL (AGED)
Mild to Medium ● Dominican Rep/Brazil ● Dominican Rep ● Connecticut Shade

Name	Length/Inches	Ring Gauge	Shape
Altamira	5	48	Robusto
Valverde	5¹/₂	42	Corona
Condado	6	50	Toro
Samana	6¹/₂	38	Panatela
Diamante	6⁵/₈	42	Lonsdale
Cabrera	7	48	Julieta

DUNHILL (SIGNED)
Medium to Full-bodied ● Dominican Rep/Colombia ● US Broadleaf ● Ecuador

Name	Length/Inches	Ring Gauge	Shape
Robusto	4¹/₂	52	Robusto
Corona	5¹/₂	42	Corona
Torpedo	5¹/₂	52	Figurado
Toro	6	50	Toro
Churchill	7	50	Julieta

Signed Churchill

1 Signed Corona **2** Signed Toro **3** Signed Robusto **4** Signed Torpedo

EL REY DEL MUNDO [CUBA/HONDURAS]

Cuban Demi-tasse

Another enduring Cuban brand, El Rey del Mundo (literally 'King of the World') is thought to have been established originally as early as 1842 by a German cigar manufacturer, Emilio Ohmstedt. However, the cigar really came to prominence when Antonio Allones took over the brand in 1882.

Don Cándido

In 1905 Cándido Vega Díaz, who was later to lend his expertise (and name) to the creation of the Dunhill house brand Don Cándido, bought the brand from Allones. In deference to the name of its best-selling cigar brand, he changed his company name from Díaz Hermanos y Cia to the El Rey del Mundo Company, and called the factory in which the cigars were produced the El Rey del Mundo factory. For a while, during the 1950s, the cigars were among the most expensive available.

Following the Cuban Revolution, the factory was renamed Héroes del Moncada, and despite nationalization the brand continued to sell well throughout the 1960s and 1970s. Production of the brand moved to the Briones Montoto factory (formerly Romeo y Julieta) when the Héroes del Moncada factory was forced to close.

Mild Cuban

Despite their dark and oily wrappers, particularly notable in the larger-sized cigars, El Rey del Mundo are considered mild for a Cuban cigar, and although the trend is for more powerful and fuller-flavoured cigars among an increasing number of cigar smokers around the world, their high-quality construction and exquisite aromas make the brand a favourite with connoisseurs. Their relatively mild taste ensures that El Reys are among the best Cuban cigars for the less-experienced smoker or for those enjoying a daytime cigar.

Although it's alleged that the famous Hollywood producer and former head of 20th Century Fox Darryl F. Zanuck favoured the Corona out of all El Rey del Mundo cigars, it is the Choix Suprême robusto that is perhaps the most celebrated among aficionados.

Honduras

The Honduran brand, of which there is a bewildering array of different vitolas, is owned by J.R. Cigars. The brand established a good reputation in its early life, primarily due to the work of Frank Llaneza (see page 128), José Orlando Padrón (see page 140) and Manuel

Zavala, all of whom brought a great deal of experience during the brand's development. Surprisingly, thanks to the use of Honduran filler and binder and an Ecuadorian wrapper, the non-Cuban brand of El Rey del Mundo cigars are fuller-bodied and spicier than the Cuban versions.

EL REY DEL MUNDO (CUBAN)

📄 Ⓢ Mild to Medium ◉ Cuba ◨ Cuba Ⓞ Cuba

Name	Length/Inches	Ring Gauge	Shape
Demi-tasse	3⁷⁄₈	30	Small Panatela
Très Petit Corona	4⁵⁄₈	43	Petit Corona
Choix Suprême	5	48	Robusto
Corona De Luxe	5¹⁄₂	42	Corona
Gran Corona	5⁵⁄₈	46	Corona Gorda
Tainos	7	47	Churchill

EL REY DEL MUNDO (HONDURAS)

📄 Ⓢ Medium to Full-bodied ◉ Honduras ◨ Honduras Ⓞ Ecuador

Name	Length/Inches	Ring Gauge	Shape
Café Noir	4¹⁄₂	35	Small Panatela
Reynitas	5	38	Short Panatela
Lew's Daytime Chest	5	44	Corona Extra
Rothschild	5	50	Robusto
Robusto Zavalla	5	54	Robusto
Rectangulares	5⁵⁄₈	45	Grand Corona
Robusto Larga	6	54	Toro
Choix Suprême	6¹⁄₈	48	Toro
Lew's Nighttime Chest	6¹⁄₄	45	Grand Corona
Flor De Lavonda	6¹⁄₂	49	Torpedo
Flor De Llaneza	6¹⁄₂	54	Torpedo
Cedars	7	43	Lonsdale
Double Corona Deluxe	7	49	Double Corona
Corona Inmensa	7¹⁄₄	47	Churchill
Robusto Suprema	7¹⁄₄	54	Double Corona
Flor Del Mundo	7¹⁄₄	54	Double Corona
1848	7⁵⁄₈	52	Double Corona
Coronation	8¹⁄₂	52	Giant

Cuban Tainos

EL REY DEL MUNDO [CONTINUED]

1 Cuban Choix Suprême

2 Cuban Gran Corona   **3** Cuban Très Petit Corona

FELIPE GREGORIO [NICARAGUA/DOMINICAN REPUBLIC]

D espite only starting his first cigar business in 1988, Philip G. Wynne has over 20 lines now appearing under his Felipe Gregorio umbrella brand. This ever-evolving brand has grown in popularity over the years, particularly in the United States.

After a brief spell in Honduras where Wynne established Petrus, his first cigar line, he moved his second fledgling brand Felipe Gregorio to Nicaragua, where he founded his own factory and started to manufacture Nicaraguan puros cigars. Wynne was asked to produce a cigar for Frank Sinatra (now in the form of the line 'Frank's Way'), with the one stipulation that it had to be made in the Dominican Republic, and so Tabacalera Real de Felipe Gregorio was established.

Felipe Gregorio cigars are at the pricier end of the scale, but consistently well made and presented. Today's lines include 809, Felipe Power (launched to celebrate the 15th anniversary of the founding of the brand), Pelo de Oro, Felipe Gregorio, Felipe II, Fusion, Felipe Felipe, Felipe Fumas, 3 Tierras, Frank's Way, the camouflaged-looking Dos & Tres Capas, Petrus Fortus, Petrus Royal Maduro, Memoria de Cuba, Gran Cuba, Regimental Colors and Premium Private Labels.

Power Obus

FELIPE GREGORIO (POWER)
Medium to Full-bodied Nicaragua Nicaragua Costa Rica

Name	Length/Inches	Ring Gauge	Shape
Petit Torpedo	4½	50	Figurado
Special R	5	52	Robusto
Leopard	5½	55	Figurado
Obus	5½	55	Toro
Triple R	5½	55	Toro
Full Power	6	60	Super Robusto
Double Corona	7½	50	Double Corona

FELIPE GREGORIO (DOMINICANA)
Medium Dominican Rep Dominican Rep Ecuador

Name	Length/Inches	Ring Gauge	Shape
Serie Especial FB	3½	55	Robusto
Serie Especial Boa	4¼	44	Figurado
Serie Especial R	4¾	54	Robusto
Serie Especial D	5½	42	Corona
Serie Especial C	5⅜	46	Corona Gorda
Serie Especial T	6	54	Toro
Serie Especial A	6½	50	Churchill

FONSECA [CUBA/DOMINICAN REPUBLIC]

Cuba No.1

Despite only having four vitolas in the brand's line-up (at time of writing), the Cuban Fonseca brand is a favourite with connoisseurs all over the world, and especially in Spain, where Fonsecas are one of the most popular premium brands.

Established in 1907 by Don Francisco Fonseca, a Spanish immigrant to Cuba, the brand is notable for the very lightweight white tissue paper wrapped around the individual cigars. This is thought to protect the wrapper and to keep the cigar at an optimal humidity level. Although rich in flavour, the cigars are mild and provide an excellent introduction for those new to Cuban cigars.

Dominican

The mild to medium Dominican Fonsecas were first produced in the late 1960s, originally using Cameroon wrappers around Dominican filler and binder. The brand was relaunched in 1991 using Connecticut Shade wrappers for the naturals, Connecticut Broadleaf for the maduros and both using Sumatra-seed binder from Mexico. Three new lines have been released recently: the 2003 individually dressed Serie F, which uses Dominican and Nicaraguan filler, Dominican binder and natural Connecticut Shade wrapper; the bolder-flavoured Sun Grown Cedar range, which utilizes Dominican binder, Dominican, Nicaraguan and Peruvian filler and a Sun Grown Connecticut wrapper, also sheathed in cedar; and finally the Vintage Collection, which has Connecticut-seed Ecuadorian shade wrappers around the perfect filler/binder combination of the best tobaccos from the Cibao Valley, Dominican Republic.

FONSECA (CUBAN)

📓 Ⓢ Mild to Medium ◉ Cuba ◑ Cuba ◯ Cuba

Name	Length/Inches	Ring Gauge	Shape
Cadetes (kdt)	4¹/₂	36	Perla
Delicias	4⁷/₈	40	Mareva
Cosacos	5¹/₄	40	Corona
No. 1	6³/₈	44	Long Corona

FONSECA (DOMINICAN)
▤ ⑤ Medium ◉ Dominican Rep ◙ Mexico
◑ Connecticut Shade (Natural)/Broadleaf (Maduro)

Name	Length/Inches	Ring Gauge	Shape
2-2 (Nat/Mad)	4¼	40	Petit Corona
5-50 (Nat/Mad)	5	50	Robusto
Triangular (Nat/Mad)	5½	56	Figurado
Toro Grande (Nat)	6	56	Grand Toro
8-9-8 (Nat)	6	43	Long Corona
7-9-9 (Nat/Mad)	6½	46	Grand Corona
10-10 (Nat/Mad)	7	50	Churchill

FONSECA (SERIE F)
▤ ⑤ Medium ◉ Dominican Rep/Nicaragua ◙ Dominican Rep
◑ Connecticut Shade

Name	Length/Inches	Ring Gauge	Shape
Breva	4¾	43	Petit Corona
Robusto	5	52	Robusto
Toro	6	50	Toro

FONSECA (SUN GROWN CEDAR)
▤ ⑤ Medium ◉ Dominican Rep/Nicaragua
◙ Dominican Rep/Nicaragua ◑ Ecuador

Name	Length/Inches	Ring Gauge	Shape
4	4¼	50	Robusto
3	5½	52	Robusto
2	6¼	52	Toro
1	6½	44	Lonsdale

FONSECA (VINTAGE)
▤ ⑤ Medium ◉ Dominican Rep ◙ Dominican Rep
◑ Ecuadorian Shader

Name	Length/Inches	Ring Gauge	Shape
Petite Belicoso	4¼	40	Petit Corona
Robusto	5	50	Robusto
Cetros	6	43	Long Corona
Belicoso	6¼	52	Belicoso
Lonsdale	6¾	45	Lonsdale
Churchill	7	50	Double Coron

Cuba Cadetes

THE GRIFFIN'S [DOMINICAN REPUBLIC]

Prestige

This brand was developed by Bernard H. Grobert in the Dominican Republic in 1964. Although the brand started life as an independent entity, it has recently come under the Davidoff umbrella. The standard Griffin's cigar is mild to medium, as can be expected from one featuring Dominican binder and filler, and a Connecticut Shade wrapper. The more fuller-flavoured Maduro series use the same filler and binder, but feature a Connecticut Broadleaf wrapper. The Fuerte range is more powerful still in response to a general trend for stronger cigars. Blended by famous cigar maker Hendrik Kelner, these feature a natural Connecticut Shade wrapper but use a more robust Dominican ligero filler.

THE GRIFFIN'S
Mild to Medium · Dominican Rep · Dominican Rep · Connecticut Shade

Name	Length/Inches	Ring Gauge	Shape
No. 500	5	42	Petit Corona
Privilege	5	32	Panatela
Pirámide	5½	52	Figurado
No. 400	6	38	Panatela
No. 300	6¼	44	Corona
Toro	6½	50	Toro
No. 100	7	38	Panatela
No. 200	7	44	Lonsdale
Prestige	7½	50	Double Corona

THE GRIFFIN'S (MADURO)
Medium to Full-bodied · Dominican Rep · Dominican Rep · Connecticut Broadleaf

Name	Length/Inches	Ring Gauge	Shape
No. 500 (Maduro)	5	42	Petit Corona
Robusto (Maduro)	5	50	Robusto
Pirámide (Maduro)	5½	52	Figurado
Toro (Maduro)	6¼	52	Toro

THE GRIFFIN'S (FUERTE)
Medium to Full-bodied · Dominican Rep · Dominican Rep · Connecticut Broadleaf

Name	Length/Inches	Ring Gauge	Shape
Fuerte Short Corona	4	43	Corona
Fuerte Robusto	4¾	48	Robusto
Fuerte Toro	6	50	Toro

HENRY CLAY [DOMINICAN REPUBLIC/HONDURAS]

N amed after the famous nineteenth-century US senator, who is believed to have owned a tobacco plantation in Cuba, Henry Clay was one of the best-known Cuban brands during the early 1900s. Following the US embargo, however, the production of Henry Clays ceased in Cuba – although the old Havana factory appears on the box.

The brand was resurrected first in the Dominican Republic, using Dominican filler and binder and a maduro Connecticut Broadleaf wrapper – with the option of being individually wrapped in Cellophane. The medium to full-bodied flavour found favour with those preferring a bolder smoke, and the cigars gained a reputation for providing good value for money despite their somewhat unattractive appearance. The Honduran Henry Clays came to life in 2005 and use a Nicaraguan binder and wrapper and a mix of Honduran, Peruvian and Nicaraguan filler leaf.

HENRY CLAY (DOMINICAN)
🗒 Ⓢ Medium to Full-bodied ◉ Dominican Rep ⬠ Dominican Rep
◒ Connecticut Broadleaf Maduro

Name	Length/Inches	Ring Gauge	Shape
Rothschild	5	50	Robusto
Brevas	5⅛	42	Corona
Breva Conservas	5⅝	46	Grand Corona
Toro	6	50	Toro
Grande	6½	48	Double Corona
Breva Finas	6½	48	Double Corona

HENRY CLAY (HONDURAN)
🗒 Ⓢ Medium ◉ Nicaragua/Honduras/Peru ⬠ Nicaragua
◒ Nicaragua

Name	Length/Inches	Ring Gauge	Shape
Hermoso	5	50	Robusto
Grande	6	50	Toro
Belicoso	6⅛	52	Figurado
Dalia	6½	44	Lonsdale
Churchill	7	52	Double Corona

Dominican Breva
Conservas

HENRY CLAY [CONTINUED]

1 Dominican Rothschild

2 Dominican Toro   **3** Dominican Brevas

H. UPMANN [CUBA/DOMINICAN REPUBLIC]

The truth behind the establishment of one of Cuba's most famous cigar brands is unclear. What is clear is that the 'Upmann' name (or possibly 'Hupmann') was that of a German banking firm active in Havana at the beginning of the nineteenth century. Legend has it that the bank provided complimentary boxes of cigars to its favoured customers; these cigars proved to be so popular that H. Upmann, the head of the Havana branch, decided in 1844 to buy a cigar factory and produce the cigars on a commercial scale – also inventing the concept of the small cedar box in which to package the cigars. The H. Upmann factory was renamed 'José Martí' following the Cuban Revolution, and still stands to this day.

Menéndez y García

Throughout the remainder of the nineteenth century and early into the twentieth century, H. Upmann cigars received accolades from around the world and grew into one of the most respected Cuban brands. In around 1922 the bank and the cigar business went bankrupt. The cigar factory and brand were bought by the British cigar importers J. Frankau & Co, who eventually sold the business in 1935 to a young Cuban

Cuban Magnum 50
EL 2005

H. UPMANN (RESERVE)
📄 Ⓢ Mild to Medium ◉ Dominican Rep/Nicaragua/Peru
🍂 Connecticut Broadleaf ◌ Ecuador

Name	Length/Inches	Ring Gauge	Shape
No. 1	5	44	Petit Corona
Lord Rothchilde	5	50	Robusto
Double Corona	6	50	Toro
No. 2	6⅛	52	Toro
Sir Winston	7	50	Double Corona

H. UPMANN (VINTAGE CAMEROON)
📄 Ⓢ Mild to Medium ◉ Dominican Rep/Nicaragua/Peru
🍂 Nicaragua ◌ Cameroon

Name	Length/Inches	Ring Gauge	Shape
Petit Corona	5	40	Petit Corona
Robusto	5	52	Robusto
Corona	5½	44	Corona
Toro	6	44	Toro
Belicoso	6⅛	52	Belicoso
Lonsdale	6⅝	44	Lonsdale
Churchill	7	50	Double Corona

Cuba Grand Corona

cigar company, Menéndez y García. Alonso Menéndez and 'Pépé' García worked hard to ensure that H. Upmann remained one of the most respected brands, and developed a new H. Upmann Montecristo Selection, which eventually became the famous Montecristo brand.

Altadis

Following the company's seizure after the Cuban Revolution, Menéndez and García opened a factory first in the Canary Islands and then later in the Dominican Republic, where today the brand is owned by Altadis.

The Cuban Upmanns are generally mild to medium and, despite some changes, are available in a wide variety of vitolas, with the Sir Winston, the Magnum 46, and the Pirámide No. 2 among the most popular. As a mark of respect to the brand, Cubatabaco released a limited edition Upmann vitola, the Magnum 50.

The Dominican Upmanns also come in a number of shapes and sizes. The last few years have seen both the Reserve series, featuring an Ecuadorian wrapper, and the Vintage Cameroon range, which marks a return to the original non-Cuban Cameroon wrapped cigars.

H. UPMANN (CUBAN)
📄 Ⓢ Mild to Medium ◉ Cuba ◙ Cuba ◌ Cuba

Name	Length/Inches	Ring Gauge	Shape
Petit Upmann	4½	36	Cadete
Corona Junior	4½	36	Cadete
Corona Minor	4⅝	40	Petit Corona
Connoisseur No. 1	5	48	Robusto
Magnum 46	5⅝	46	Corona Gorda
Magnum 50 EL 2005	6⅕	50	Double Robusto
Grand Corona	5¾	40	Corona
Pírámide No. 2	6⅛	52	Figurado
Sir Winston/Monarca	7	47	Julieta

H. UPMANN (DOMINICAN)
📄 Ⓢ Mild to Medium ◉ Dominican Rep/Brazil ◙ Dominican Rep ◌ Indonesia

Name	Length/Inches	Ring Gauge	Shape
Demi-tasse	4½	33	Demi-tasse
Petit Corona	5	44	Petit Corona
No. 100	5	50	Robusto
Lonsdale	6½	44	Lonsdale
Toro	6	50	Toro
Belicoso	6⅛	52	Belicoso

1 Cuban Corona Minor (Tubo) **2** Cuban Sir Winston
3 Cuban Magnum 46 **4** Cuban Corona Junior

HOYO DE MONTERREY [CUBA/HONDURAS]

Honduran Demi-Tasse

The Hoyo de Monterrey brand was established in 1865 by a former tobacco farmer, José Gener. Gener had learned the tobacco trade as a young man working on a plantation near the village of San Juan y Martinez, in the Vuelta Abajo region of Cuba, the location of the country's finest tobacco plantations. In the village, an iron gate still features the words 'Hoyo de Monterrey: José Gener 1860'. Made at the Fernando Roig factory (formerly La Corona), Hoyo de Monterreys – noticeably the Double Corona (which is now almost legendary) but also the Epicures Nos. 1 & 2 have – over the years – established themselves as favourites with aficionados. Nor should it be forgotten that Zino Davidoff based his celebrated Châteaux series around the cabinet selection Hoyo de Monterrey. Also notable within the brand is the Le Hoyo range, which first appeared in 1970.

HOYO DE MONTERREY (CUBAN)
📋 🍂 Mild to Medium ⦿ Cuba 🍂 Cuba ◯ Cuba

Name	Length/Inches	Ring Gauge	Shape
Le Hoyo du Depute	4¼	38	Perla
Margarita	4¾	26	Cigarillo
Epicure No. 2	4⅞	50	Robusto
Le Hoyo du Prince	5	40	Mareva
Short Hoyo Corona	5	42	Mareva
Le Hoyo du Roi	5½	42	Corona
Epicure No. 1	5⅝	46	Corona Gorda
Le Hoyo du Dauphin	6	38	Laguito No. 2
Le Hoyo des Dieux	6	42	Corona Grande
Double Corona	7⅝	49	Double Corona
Particulares LE 2001	9¼	47	Gran Corona

HOYO DE MONTERREY (HONDURAN)
📋 🍂 Full-bodied ⦿ Dominican Rep/Honduras/Nicaragua
🍂 Connecticut Broadleaf ◯ Ecuador

Name	Length/Inches	Ring Gauge	Shape
Demi-Tasse	4	39	Demi-Tasse
Rothschild	4½	50	Robusto
Margarita	5¼	29	Cigarillo
Super Hoyo	5½	44	Corona
Corona	5⅝	46	Corona
Churchill	6¼	45	Grand Corona
Double Corona	6¾	48	Double Corona
Largo Elegante	7¼	34	Long Panatela
Presidente	8½	52	Giant

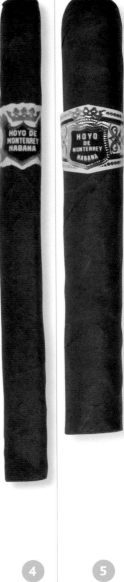

1 Cuban Limited Edition Particulares 2001

2 Cuban Double Corona

3 Cuban Le Hoyo du Prince **4** Cuban Margarita

5 Cuban Le Hoyo du Depute

Honduras

The Honduran Hoyo de Monterrey brand was established in 1965, along with Honduran Punch. Both brands were originally owned by Fernando Palicio in Cuba, who was forced to give them up to Castro following the Revolution. As his final act, Palicio sold the US rights of the brands to Villazon & Co., now a subsidiary of General Cigar Co. Initially, the US-owned Hoyo brand was manufactured in Tampa, Florida, but under the legendary and highly influential Frank Llaneza (who would later rise to be president of Villazon) production moved to Honduras in 1969.

Llaneza, and later Estelo Padrón, worked wonders with the Hoyo brand, creating full-bodied and punchy cigars, using filler from Nicaragua, the Dominican Republic and Honduras, US Broadleaf binder and Ecuadorian Sumatra-seed wrappers. Particularly popular was the Excalibur series (marketed as a brand in its own right in Europe), which utilised Connecticut Shade wrapper; more recently Hoyo have released the even more robust Dark Sumatran line.

Cuba Epicure No. 2

HOYO DE MONTERREY (DARK SUMATRA)
📄 Ⓢ Full-bodied ◉ Dominican Rep/Honduras/Nicaragua
◉ Connecticut Broadleaf Ⓞ Ecuador

Name	Length/Inches	Ring Gauge	Shape
Espresso	4½	50	Robusto
Media Noche	5¾	54	Toro
Ebano	6	45	Grand Corona
Noche	6½	52	Toro

HOYO DE MONTERREY (EXCALIBUR 1066)
📄 Ⓢ Full-bodied ◉ Dominican Rep/Honduras/Nicaragua
◉ Ecuador/Connecticut Broadleaf Ⓞ Connecticut Shade/Cameroon

Name	Length/Inches	Ring Gauge	Shape
Merlin	5¼	50	Robusto
King Arthur	6¼	45	Corona
Galahad	6¾	47	Churchill
Lancelot	7¼	54	Double Corona

LA GLORIA CUBANA

[CUBA/DOMINICAN REPUBLIC/UNITED STATES]

lthough established in 1885 and a popular export brand during the mid-nineteenth century, La Gloria Cubana is perhaps one of the lesser-known Cuban brands. Much of this can be put down to the fact that shortly after the Revolution production of the brand stopped entirely, and it was only in 1967 that the brand was brought back to life, although rolled in relatively small numbers. Known for its long slim panatelas, the brand is made at the Partagás factory, but the cigars are generally considered lighter than the Partagás brand, although the Medaille d'Or No. 2 has won respect from aficionados the world over.

Ernesto Perez-Carrillo

The former Cuban senator and tobacco farmer, Ernesto Perez-Carrillo, took La Gloria Cubana's blending notes with him when he left Cuba in

LA GLORIA CUBANA (CUBAN)

📄 ⑤ Medium ◉ Cuba ◪ Cuba ◯ Cuba

Name	Length/Inches	Ring Gauge	Shape
Medaille d'Or No. 4	6	32	Panatela
Medaille d'Or No. 2	6¾	43	Dalia
Medaille d'Or No. 3	6⅞	28	Panatela Larga
Taino	7	47	Julieta
Medaille d'Or No. 1	7¼	36	Delicado Extra

LA GLORIA CUBANA (DOMINICAN/US)

📄 ⑤ Medium to Full-bodied ◉ Dominican Rep/Nicaragua
◪ Nicaragua ◯ Ecuador

Name	Length/Inches	Ring Gauge	Shape
Wavell	5	50	Robusto
Torpedo No. 1	6½	54	Figurado
Panatela Deluxe	7	37	Long Panatela
Medaille d'Or No. 4	6	32	Panatela
Corona Gorda	6	52	Toro
Medaille d'Or No. 2	6¼	43	Long Corona
Gloria Extra	6¼	46	Grand Corona
Medaille d'Or No. 1	6¾	43	Lonsdale
Medaille d'Or No. 3	7	33	Long Panatela
Churchill	7	50	Churchill
Gloria Immenso	7¾	48	Churchill
Soberano	8	52	Giant
Crown Imperial	9	49	Giant

Cuban
Medaille d'Or No. 2

Cuban Taino

1959 following the Revolution, and began making the cigars in Little Havana, Miami, in the late 1960s. Their unusually full flavour, which became even stronger in the 1980s when Ernesto Jr began blending stronger Dominican and Nicaraguan leaf, ensured their popularity, and to keep up with demand the Carrillo family established a second factory in the Dominican Republic while retaining the US operation. After his father's death, Ernesto Jr continued to create even fuller-bodied cigars in the form of the Serie R line, which is available in natural and maduro wrappers, and despite retaining the day-to-day running of the company he sold the brand to the Swedish tobacco giant Swedish Match for several millions of dollars. In 2005 the Reserva Figurados line was introduced which uses Dominican and Nicaraguan filler, Nicaraguan binder and either an Ecuadorian natural wrapper or a Connecticut Broadleaf maduro.

As well as their rich aromas and powerful flavours La Gloria Cubana cigars are also notable for their good construction, with the Torpedo No. 1 in particular gaining favour with cigar lovers the world over for its remarkably good shape.

LA GLORIA CUBANA (SERIE R)
📄 💲 Medium to Full-bodied ◉ Dominican Rep/Nicaragua
◪ Nicaragua ◖ Ecuador

Name	Length/Inches	Ring Gauge	Shape
No. 4	4⅞	52	Robusto
No. 5	5½	54	Robusto
No. 6	5⅞	60	Robusto
No. 7	7	58	Double Corona

LA GLORIA CUBANA (RESERVA FIGURADOS)
📄 💲 Medium to Full-bodied ◉ Dominican Rep/Nicaragua
◪ Nicaragua ◖ Ecuador/Connecticut Broadleaf

Name	Length/Inches	Ring Gauge	Shape
Felicias	4⅝	49	Figurado
Flechas Especiales	6	49	Figurado
Regalias Perfecto	6¼	57	Figurado
Pirámides Classicas	7	56	Figurado
Selectos de Lujos	7	54	Figurado

MACANUDO [DOMINICAN REPUBLIC]

T he Macanudo brand is one of the best-selling premium
cigar brands in the United States. The name 'Macanudo'
(colloquial Spanish for 'great' or 'super') was first used in
relation to cigars as a name for a particular Cuban Punch before
World War II. At that time Punch was owned by the Palicio family,
and they, along with other Cuban families, settled in Jamaica at
the outset of the war, where they established Macanudo as a
brand in its own right.

The Macanudo brand was first introduced to the United States in
1970 by General Cigar Co. Their smooth, mild flavours and excellent
construction made them the best-selling brand in the United States.

MACANUDO (CAFÉ)
📋 🚫 Mild to Medium ◉ Dominican Rep/Mexico 🚫 Mexico
⬙ Connecticut Shade

Name	Length/Inches	Ring Gauge	Shape
Caviar	4	36	Small Panatela
Ascot	4³/₁₆	32	Small Panatela
Lords	4³/₄	49	Robusto
Petit Corona	5	38	Petit Corona
Duke of Devon	5½	42	Corona
Crystal	5½	50	Robusto
Duke of Windsor	6	50	Toro
Majesty	6	54	Toro
Baron de Rothschild	6½	42	Lonsdale
Trump	6½	45	Toro
Portofino	7	34	Long Panatela
898	7	45	Grand Corona
Prince of Wales	8	52	Giant
Duke of Wellington	8½	47	Giant

MACANUDO (ROBUST)
📋 🚫 Medium ◉ Dominican Rep/Honduras/Nicaragua
🚫 Connecticut Broadleaf ⬙ Connecticut Shade

Name	Length/Inches	Ring Gauge	Shape
Ascot	4³/₁₆	32	Small Panatela
Petit Corona	5	38	Petit Corona
Duke of Devon	5½	42	Corona
Hyde Park	5½	49	Robusto
Hampton Court	5½	42	Corona
Baron de Rothschild	6½	42	Long Corona
Portofino	7	34	Long Panatela
Prince Philip	7½	49	Double Corona

Café Duke of Windsor

Maduro Diplomat

For around 30 years the brand was made in Jamaica's Temple Hall factory and production also started in the Dominican Republic. The Jamaican factory closed in 2000, and the cigars are now made exclusively in the Dominican Republic.

There are five lines – the classic Macanudo Café, and the Robust, Maduro, Vintage and Gold Label series. All use Connecticut Shade wrappers apart from the Maduros, which use Connecticut Broadleaf. The Gold Label series use golden 1st and 2nd primings, while the Vintage selection uses 1997 vintage Shade wrappers. Depending on the series, the fillers come from Mexico, the Dominican Republic (Cuban-seed), Nicaragua and Honduras.

MACANUDO (MADURO)
📖 🚬 Medium ◉ Dominican Rep/Mexico 🌿 Connecticut Broadleaf ◖ Connecticut Broadleaf

Name	Length/Inches	Ring Gauge	Shape
Ascot	4³⁄₁₆	32	Small Panatela
Diplomat	4½	60	Figurado
Hyde Park	5½	49	Robusto
Hampton Court	5½	42	Corona
Duke of Devon	5½	42	Corona
Baron de Rothschild	6½	42	Long Corona
Prince Philip	7½	49	Double Corona

MACANUDO (VINTAGE)
📖 🚬 Medium ◉ Dominican Rep/Mexico 🌿 Mexico ◖ Connecticut Shade (1997)

Name	Length/Inches	Ring Gauge	Shape
Demi 97	4³⁄₁₆	36	Short Panatela
VIII	5½	50	Robusto
V	5½	49	Robusto
III	5½	43	Corona
II	6½	43	Long Corona
I	7½	49	Double Corona

MACANUDO (GOLD LABEL)
📖 🚬 Medium ◉ Dominican Rep/Mexico 🌿 Mexico ◖ Golden Connecticut Shade

Name	Length/Inches	Ring Gauge	Shape
Somerset	5	54	Robusto
Duke of York	5¼	54	Robusto
Tudor	6	52	Toro
Shakespeare	6½	45	Grand Corona
Lord Nelson	7	49	Churchill

MONTECRISTO [CUBA/DOMINICAN REPUBLIC]

Accounting for around 50 per cent of premium Cuban cigar exports, the Montecristo brand is probably the best-known premium cigar in the world. The No. 4 is believed to outsell any other Cuban premium cigar, while the Montecristo No. 2 (pyramid) is regarded by many as one of the finest Cuban cigars of all time.

The brand was created in 1935 by (Alonso) Menéndez y (Pépé) García, who had in the same year acquired H. Upmann from the English cigar importers J. Frankau & Co. Menéndez and García wanted to extend the Upmann range, and so was born the H. Upmann Montecristo Selection – a line of only five vitolas ranging from the No. 1 Cervantes (or Lonsdale) through to the No. 5 Petit Corona. Legend has it that the name was taken from the novel by Alexandre Dumas, *The Count of Monte Cristo*, which was a favourite of the *torcedores* at the H. Upmann factory at the time. The new Montecristo range was marketed and sold exclusively through the prestigious Dunhill shops, and quickly established itself as a superior brand around the world; Alfred Hitchcock was among its fans.

MONTECRISTO (CLASSIC)
📄 Ⓢ Medium ◉ Dominican Rep ◉ Dominican Rep
◗ Connecticut Shade

Name	Length/Inches	Ring Gauge	Shape
No. 5	4	40	Petit Corona
No. 4	5	40	Petit Corona
Robusto	5	52	Robusto
Especial No. 3	5½	44	Corona
Toro	6	52	Toro
No. 2	6⅛	52	Belicoso
Especial No. 1	6⅝	44	Grand Corona
Churchill	7	54	Double Corona

Cuban Edmundo

MONTECRISTO (PLATINUM)
📄 Ⓢ Medium ◉ Dominican Rep/Nicaragua/Peru ◉ Nicaragua
◗ Mexico

Name	Length/Inches	Ring Gauge	Shape
Robusto	5	50	Robusto
No. 3	5½	44	Corona
Toro	6	50	Toro
Habana No. 2	6⅛	52	Belicoso
No. 1	6½	44	Lonsdale

Cuban No. 4

José Manuel González

The original five-vitola line-up remained unchanged after World War II, with the exception of the Tubo, which was added in the 1940s. José Manuel González took over control of the Montecristo brand after the Revolution had forced Menéndez and García to leave Cuba for the Canary Islands and then the Dominican Republic. Under his now legendary supervision in the 1970s four more cigars were introduced. They were the 9-inch Montecristo 'A', the Especial, the Especial No. 2 and the Joyitas – these last three being Laguito Nos. 1, 2 and 3 vitolas (the same sizes as the flagship Cohíba brand). These additions to the brand, which also featured the trademark medium to full body and unique spice flavours, helped to reinforce Montecristo as the leading Cuban cigar. They were later joined by the Petit Tubo, and then the Montecristo 'B', No. 6 and No. 7. In 2004 a new vitola was created, the Edmundo, and a number of limited edition releases including the 2006 Robusto – a limited edition maduro.

MONTECRISTO (CUBAN)
📖 ⑤ Medium to Full-bodied ◉ Cuba ⚫ Cuba ◯ Cuba

Name	Length/Inches	Ring Gauge	Shape
No. 5	4	40	Perla
Joyitas	4½	26	Laguito No. 3
No. 4	5	42	Mareva
Robusto LE 2006	5	52	Robusto
Edmundo	5¼	52	Robusto
No. 3	5½	42	Corona
Montecristo 'C'	5½	46	Corona Gorda
Especial No. 2	6	38	Laguito No. 2
No. 2	6	52	Figurado
No. 1	6½	42	Cervante
Montecristo 'D' 898	6¾	43	Dalia
Especial No. 1	7½	38	Laguito No. 1
Montecristo 'A'	9¼	47	Grand Corona

MONTECRISTO (DOMINICAN)
📖 ⑤ Mild to Medium ◉ Dominican Rep ⚫ Dominican Rep ◯ Connecticut Shade

Name	Length/Inches	Ring Gauge	Shape
Robusto	4¾	50	Robusto
No. 3	5½	44	Corona
No. 2	6	50	Figurado
Double Corona	6¼	50	Double Corona
No. 1	6½	44	Lonsdale
Churchill	7	50	Churchill

1 Cuban Montecristo 'A' 2 Cuban No. 2 3 Cuban Robusto LE 2006
4 Cuban Joyitas

Dominican
Double Corona

Altadis USA

The Dominican Montecristo brand was launched in earnest in 1995, since when it has become one of the leaders in America and a commercial success for its owner Altadis USA. Generally mild to medium, Dominican Montecristos are available as Montecristo, Classic, Platinum, Serie C or White. The first two feature natural Connecticut Shade wrappers; the Platinum uses a distinctive Mexican Cuban-seed wrapper; the Serie C has wrappers from Cameroon; while the White features Ecuadorian Connecticut Shade. Depending on the series, binders and fillers come from Nicaragua, the Dominican Republic and Peru.

MONTECRISTO (SERIES C)

Medium · Dominican Rep/Nicaragua/Peru · Nicaragua · Cameroon

Name	Length/Inches	Ring Gauge	Shape
Corona	5½	44	Corona
Robusto	5	52	Robusto
Toro	6	54	Toro
Belicoso	6⅛	52	Belicoso

MONTECRISTO (WHITE)

Medium · Dominican Rep/Nicaragua · Nicaragua · Ecuador

Name	Length/Inches	Ring Gauge	Shape
Rothchilde	5	52	Robusto
Especial No. 3	5½	44	Corona
Toro	6	54	Toro
No. 2 Belicoso	6⅛	52	Belicoso
Especial No. 1	6½	44	Lonsdale
Churchill	7	54	Churchill

MONTESINO [DOMINICAN REPUBLIC]

T he Montesino brand of cigars was one of the first to be created by Carlos Fuente when he established his now vast cigar empire in the Dominican Republic in 1980. Originally the brand was made in only four sizes, available in either a natural Connecticut Shade wrapper or a maduro Connecticut Broadleaf wrapped around aged filler and binder from the Dominican Republic. More recently, thanks to a greater stock of aged tobaccos and as more rollers have been trained, along with the original Gran Corona, the No. 1 and No. 2, and the popular Diplomatico, further vitolas have been added to the line, including a pirámide that features an Ecuadorian wrapper.

Undiscovered Montesino

Despite winning plaudits around the world, and having a reputation as consistently well-made yet inexpensive cigars, Montesinos have struggled to win the same sort of acclaim enjoyed by Arturo Fuente and OpusX cigars, the big hitters for Tabacalera A. Fuente y Cia.

Robusto

MONTESINO
▤ Ⓢ Medium ◉ Dominican Rep/Nicaragua ◉ Dominican Rep
◐ Ecuador

Name	Length/Inches	Ring Gauge	Shape
Robusto	5	50	Robusto
Belicoso Magnum	5¼	52	Belicoso
Diplomatico	5½	42	Corona
Belicoso No. 2	6	49	Belicoso
Toro	6	50	Toro
Pirámide	6	52	Figurado
No. 2	6¼	44	Long Corona
Gran Corona	6¾	48	Churchill
Super Belicoso	6¾	54	Double Corona
No. 1	6⅞	43	Lonsdale

NAT SHERMAN [DOMINICAN REPUBLIC]

Metropolitan
University

F ew cigar lovers who have visited New York over the years will have passed up the opportunity to visit the famous Nat Sherman tobacco store. Nat Sherman opened his first store on Broadway in 1930, in partnership with Charles Baer, owner of the Epoca Cigar Factory. Sherman bought out Baer soon after, and so began the family business that remains today. During World War II he began to create his own cigar labels, which for the next 60 years were smoked in Gentlemen's Clubs throughout Manhattan. Historically, Nat Sherman cigars have embraced the culture of New York.

NAT SHERMAN (HOST)
Mild to Medium Dominican Rep Dominican Rep Connecticut Shade

Name	Length/Inches	Ring Gauge	Shape
Hudson	4¾	32	Small Panatela
Hobart	5	50	Robusto
Hamilton	5½	42	Corona
Hunter	6	43	Long Corona
Harrington	6	48	Toro
Hampton	7	50	Double Corona

NAT SHERMAN (METROPOLITAN)
Mild to Medium Dominican Rep Dominican Rep Connecticut Shade

Name	Length/Inches	Ring Gauge	Shape
Union	4½	50	Robusto
Banker	5	70	Super Robusto
Angler	5½	43	Figurado
University	6	50	Toro
Explorer	6½	52	Belicoso
Metropolitan	7	50	Double Corona

NAT SHERMAN (METROPOLITAN MADURO)
Mild to Medium Dominican Rep Dominican Rep Connecticut Broadleaf

Name	Length/Inches	Ring Gauge	Shape
Union	4½	50	Robusto
Banker	5	70	Super Robusto
Angler	5½	43	Figurado
University	6	50	Toro
Explorer	6½	52	Belicoso
Metropolitan	7	50	Double Corona

At present there are eight Nat Sherman own-brand lines: Host, Metropolitan, Metropolitan Maduro, VIP, Gotham Eastside, Gotham Westside, the 1400 and Suave. There's a Nat Sherman cigar for everyone, and the various selections use a wide range of tobaccos including fillers and binders from South America and the Dominican Republic and maduro or natural wrappers mostly from Connecticut.

Metropolitan
Metropolitan

NAT SHERMAN (VIP)

📄 ⑤ Medium ◉ Dominican Rep ◐ Dominican Rep/South America ◯ Connecticut Shade

Name	Length/Inches	Ring Gauge	Shape
Vanderbilt	4½	40	Petit Corona
Astor	4½	50	Robusto
Carnegie	6	48	Toro
Morgan	7	42	Churchill
Zigfeld	7	50	Double Corona

NAT SHERMAN (GOTHAM EASTSIDE)

📄 ⑤ Mild to Medium ◉ Dominican Rep ◐ Dominican Rep ◯ Connecticut Shade

Name	Length/Inches	Ring Gauge	Shape
No. 175	5	42	Petit Corona
No. 65	6	32	Slim Panatela
No. 711	6	50	Toro
No. 1440	6¼	44	Long Corona
No. 500	7	50	Double Corona
No. 629	6	59	Belicoso

NAT SHERMAN (GOTHAM WESTSIDE)

📄 ⑤ Mild to Medium ◉ Dominican Rep/Peru ◐ Dominican Rep/Peru ◯ Brazil

Name	Length/Inches	Ring Gauge	Shape
No. 175	5	42	Petit Corona
No. 65	6	32	Slim Panatela
No. 711	6	50	Toro
No. 1440	6¼	44	Long Corona
No. 500	7	50	Double Corona
No. 629	6	59	Belicoso

NAT SHERMAN (1400)

📄 ⑤ Medium ◉ Nicaragua ◐ Nicaragua ◯ Ecuador

Name	Length/Inches	Ring Gauge	Shape
Palma Grande	6½	44	Lonsdale
Double Corona	7	50	Double Corona

PADRON [NICARAGUA/HONDURAS]

2000

The story of Padrón cigars is a real-life rags-to-riches tale. Thirty-seven-year-old José Orlando Padrón left Cuba following the Revolution, leaving his family's prime tobacco plantation in Pinar del Río and settling in Miami, Florida, without a cent to his name. With some money from a Cuban relief fund and a loan from a friend, he set about earning his living mowing lawns in the Miami area. In his spare time Padrón, along with the help of one roller, began producing cigars; their popularity among the local inhabitants quickly spread and he established the Padrón brand in 1964.

By 1970, having discovered a Cuban-seed Nicaraguan tobacco, which he felt was closer to Cuban tobacco than anything else he'd encountered, Padrón established a factory in Nicaragua. A brief period of growth was snuffed out by the growing civil unrest caused by the struggle between the emerging Sandinistas and the Somoza government in 1978. Undeterred, Padrón moved across the border to Honduras in 1979, where he opened another factory.

Anniversary Series

Over the years Padrón's attention to detail, his love of growing the highest-quality tobacco and ageing it with the utmost care and patience, has seen him produce cigars (most are available in both

PADRON
Medium   Nicaragua   Nicaragua   Nicaragua

Name	Length/Inches	Ring Gauge	Shape
Delicias	4⁷⁄₈	46	Corona Extra
2000	5	50	Robusto
Chicos	5½	36	Panatela
Londres	5½	42	Corona
3000	5½	52	Robusto
5000	5½	56	Toro
Palmas	6⁵⁄₁₆	42	Lonsdale
4000	6½	54	Churchill
Panatela	6⁷⁄₈	36	Panatela
Ambassador	6⁷⁄₈	42	Lonsdale
Churchill	6⁷⁄₈	46	Churchill
Executive	7½	50	Double Corona
Grand Reserve	8	41	Long Corona
Magnum	9	50	Giant

natural and maduro wrappers) that score consistently highly in blind tastings the world over; his business has grown proportionately as a result. In 1994, to celebrate the company's 30th anniversary, the family created the Padrón 1964 Anniversary Series, which utilized filler tobacco that had been aged for at least four years. This series, which features nine vitolas also available in either natural or maduro wrappers, was an instant hit. This was followed up with a limited edition 'Millennium Series' cigar (a 6-inch x 52-ring toro), in which not only were the 1,000 boxes individually and sequentially numbered, but so, too, were the 100 cigars that each contained. These were followed in 2004 by the Serie 1926 (to honour the year in which José Orlando Padrón was born), the natural wrapper version of which was voted *Cigar Aficionados'* Cigar of the Year. The company is soon to release its 40th Anniversary cigars, which are based around the Serie 1926.

PADRON (1964 ANNIVERSARY SERIES)

📄 Ⓢ Medium to Full-bodied ◉ Nicaragua ▨ Nicaragua
◯ Nicaragua

Name	Length/Inches	Ring Gauge	Shape
Príncipe	4½	46	Corona Extra
2000	5	50	Robusto
Exclusivo	5½	50	Robusto
Corona	6	42	Long Corona
Torpedo	6	52	Belicoso
Imperial	6	54	Toro
Superior	6½	42	Lonsdale
Monarcha	6½	46	Grand Corona
Pirámide	6⅞	42	Figurado
Diplomatico	7	50	Double Corona
'A'	8¾	50	Corona Extra

PADRON (SERIE 1926)

📄 Ⓢ Medium to Full-bodied ◉ Nicaragua ▨ Nicaragua
◯ Nicaragua

Name	Length/Inches	Ring Gauge	Shape
No. 35	4	48	Robusto
No. 6	4¾	50	Robusto
No. 9	5¼	56	Robusto
No. 2	5½	52	Belicoso
No. 40	6½	54	Figurado
No. 1	6¾	54	Double Corona

1964 Anniversary
Series Torpedo

PARTAGAS [CUBA/DOMINICAN REPUBLIC]

Cuban Short

Another Cuban brand that has passed into folklore, Partagás was established in 1845 by Don Jaime Partagás Ravelo, making it one of the oldest Havana brands. Partagás had moved to Cuba from Spain around 1825, and in a relatively short space of time began to buy up plantations in Cuba's prime tobacco-growing region of Vuelta Abajo and to produce well-respected cigars. His cigar business went from strength to strength, culminating in the building of the now famous Partagás factory in 1845 (it was known as Francisco Perez German following the Revolution) and the establishment of the brand.

Following Don Jaime's death in the latter half of the 1860s – he was allegedly killed over an affair of the heart – his son José Partagás took control of the business. José sold the business to the banker José Bances in 1900, who in turn sold the firm to Fernández

PARTAGAS (LIMITED RESERVE)
📄 Ⓢ Medium ◉ Dominican Rep/Mexico ◎ Mexico
◯ Cameroon

Name	Length/Inches	Ring Gauge	Shape
Epicure	5	38	Short Panatela
Robusto	5½	49	Robusto
Regale	6½	47	Grand Corona
Royale	6¾	43	Long Corona

PARTAGAS (SPANISH ROSADO)
📄 Ⓢ Medium ◉ Dominican Rep/Mexico/Honduras
◎ Connecticut Broadleaf ◯ Honduras

Name	Length/Inches	Ring Gauge	Shape
Rojito	4½	50	Robusto
San Augustin	5½	52	Robusto
Familia	6	54	Toro
Ramón y Ramón	6½	45	Grand Corona
Mitico	7	49	Double Corona

PARTAGAS (CIFUENTES)
📄 Ⓢ Medium to Full-bodied ◉ Nicaragua ◎ Nicaragua
◯ Honduras

Name	Length/Inches	Ring Gauge	Shape
Septiembre	5½	49	Robusto
Octobre	6	54	Toro
Noviembre	6½	45	Grand Corona

y Cifuentes, a partnership of two well-established cigar families. On Fernández's departure from the company, Cifuentes went into partnership with Francisco Pego, and as Cifuentes y Pego they also acquired the rights to the well-respected if little-known Ramón Allones brand. In 1954 the brand and factory passed into the control of Ramón Cifuentes, who acquired the rights to the Bolívar and La Gloria Cubana brands. He proceeded to produce these at the Partagás factory, making it the second-largest exporter of premium cigars after the H. Upmann factory.

Today the Partagás factory is one of the main destinations for tourists interested in cigars. Partagás produce full-bodied cigars in a large array of sizes. Among the best known are the Serie D No.

PARTAGAS (DOMINICAN)

📄 ⑤ Medium ◉ Dominican Rep/Mexico ◉ Mexico
◯ Cameroon

Name	Length/Inches	Ring Gauge	Shape
Robusto	4½	49	Robusto
No. 4	5	38	Short Panatela
Naturales	5½	50	Robusto
No. 2	5¾	43	Corona
Sabroso	5⅞	44	Long Corona
Aristocrat	6	50	Belicoso
Fabuloso	7	52	Double Corona
No. 9	8½	47	Giant

PARTAGAS (BLACK LABEL)

📄 ⑤ Medium ◉ Dominican Rep ◉ Dominican Rep/Nicaragua
◯ Connecticut Broadleaf

Name	Length/Inches	Ring Gauge	Shape
Bravo	4½	54	Robusto
Maximo	6	50	Toro
Magnifico	6	54	Toro
Pirámide	6	60	Figurado

PARTAGAS (SERIE S)

📄 ⑤ Medium ◉ Dominican Rep/Mexico ◉ Mexico
◯ Cameroon

Name	Length/Inches	Ring Gauge	Shape
Esplendido	4½	60	Figurado
Preferido	6	52	Belicoso
Perfecto	6	49	Figurado
Primero	6	60	Figurado
Exquisito	7¼	54	Figurado

Cuban 8-9-8

4 (Robusto), the Serie D No. 3 2001 Limited Edition (re-released in 2006) and the 8-9-8 Dalia.

Dominican

Ramón Cifuentes left Cuba in 1961, two years after the Revolution, and the Partagás factory was nationalized. In 1974 Ramón sold a share of the US rights to the Partagás brand to General Cigar Company, and under his supervision non-Cuban Partagás cigars were manufactured in Jamaica. The factory was relocated to the Dominican Republic in 1979. Initially, the cigars were notable for the use of a rich Cameroon wrapper, which is still used in the Partagás, Serie S and Limited Reserve lines. More recently, trends for fuller-bodied cigars have seen the brand using Honduran wrappers and more powerful filler blends in both their Spanish Rosado and Partagás Cifuentes series (the latter named after Ramón, who died in 2000). The Black Label line uses a Connecticut wrapper.

PARTAGAS (CUBA)

Full-bodied Cuba Cuba Cuba

Name	Length/Inches	Ring Gauge	Shape
Short	$4^3/_{10}$	42	Petit Corona
Serie D No. 4	$4^7/_8$	50	Robusto
Habaneros	5	39	Belvederas
Petit Corona Especial	5	44	Petit Corona
Corona	$5^1/_2$	42	Corona
Serie D No. 3 LE 2006	$5^3/_5$	46	Corona Gorda
Super Partagás	6	40	Nacionales
Serie D No. 2 LE 2003	6	50	Toro
Serie P No. 2	6	52	Pirámide
De Partagás No. 1	$6^3/_5$	43	Dalia
8-9-8	$6^3/_4$	43	Dalia
Churchill De Luxe	7	47	Julieta
Lusitania	$7^5/_8$	49	Prominent

Cuban Lusitania

1 Cuban Serie D No. 4 **2** Cuban Serie P No. 2 **3** Cuban Serie D No. 3 LE 2006

PAUL GARMIRIAN (PG) [DOMINICAN REPUBLIC]

Gourmet Epicure

Established in 1990, PG cigars are among the finest to come out of the Dominican Republic. The Gourmet Series features Connecticut Shade wrappers and fillers, and binders from the Dominican Republic. Available in 21 vitolas, it has spicy yet smooth flavours, and is medium strength. The more recent Gourmet Series II is fuller bodied than the original. The Reserva Exclusiva line is even stronger, featuring ten-year-old tobacco comprising Dominican and Ecuadorian filler, Dominican binder and Ecuadorian wrapper. The Gourmet Maduro Series uses Dominican and Brazilian filler, Indonesian binder and Connecticut Broadleaf wrapper.

PAUL GARMIRIAN (GOURMET)
📄 🚬 Medium to Full-bodied ◉ Dominican Rep ◐ Dominican Rep
◐ Connecticut Shade

Name	Length/Inches	Ring Gauge	Shape
Bombones	3½	43	Petit Corona
No. 5	4	40	Petit Corona
Torito	4	50	Robusto
Petit Bouquet	4½	38	Belicoso
No. 2	4¾	48	Robusto
Petit Corona	5	43	Petit Corona
Robusto	5	50	Robusto
Corona	5½	42	Corona
Epicure	5½	50	Robusto
Belicoso Fino	5½	52	Belicoso
Especial	5¾	38	Panatela
Connoisseur	6	50	Toro
Lonsdale	6½	42	Lonsdale
Corona Grande	6½	46	Grand Corona
No. 1	7½	38	Long Panatela

PAUL GARMIRIAN (GOURMET MADURO)
📄 🚬 Medium to Full-bodied ◉ Dominican Rep/Brazil
◐ Indonesia ◐ Connecticut Broadleaf

Name	Length/Inches	Ring Gauge	Shape
Bombones Maduro	3½	43	Petit Corona
Torito Maduro	4	50	Robusto
Robusto Maduro	5	50	Robusto
Connoisseur Maduro	6	50	Toro
Belicoso Maduro	6¼	52	Belicoso
Magnum Maduro	7	50	Double Corona
Celebration Maduro	9	50	Giant

PAUL GARMIRIAN (GOURMET 15TH ANNIVERSARY)

📋 ⑤ Medium to Full-bodied ◉ Dominican Rep ◎ Dominican Rep
◐ Colorado/Nicaragua

Name	Length/Inches	Ring Gauge	Shape
Robusto	5	50	Robusto
Corona Extra	5½	46	Corona Extra
Belicoso Extra	6¾	52	Belicoso
Connoisseur	6	52	Toro

PAUL GARMIRIAN (RESERVA EXCLUSIVA)

📋 ⑤ Medium to Full-bodied ◉ Dominican Rep/Ecuador
◎ Dominican Rep ◐ Ecuador

Name	Length/Inches	Ring Gauge	Shape
No. 5 RE	4	40	Petit Corona
Torito RE	4	50	Robusto
Corona Extra RE	5	46	Corona Extra
Robusto RE	5	50	Robusto
Corona RE	5½	42	Corona
Connoisseur RE	6	50	Toro
Belicoso RE	6¼	52	Belicoso
Churchill RE	7	48	Churchill
Gran Panatela RE	7½	40	Long Panatela

PAUL GARMIRIAN (ARTISAN'S SELECTION)

📋 ⑤ Mild to Medium ◉ Dominican Rep ◎ Dominican Rep
◐ Connecticut Shade

Name	Length/Inches	Ring Gauge	Shape
No. 7	4½	48	Robusto
No. 3	5	50	Robusto
No. 5	5	52	Belicoso
No. 9	5¼	42	Corona
No. 4	5½	52	Belicoso
No. 2	6	50	Toro
No. 8	6¼	46	Grand Corona
No. 6	7	48	Churchill
No. 1	7½	50	Double Corona

PAUL GARMIRIAN (GOURMET II)

📋 ⑤ Full-bodied ◉ Dominican Rep ◎ Dominican Rep
◐ Connecticut Shade

Name	Length/Inches	Ring Gauge	Shape
Robusto	5	50	Robusto
Belicoso Fino	5½	52	Belicoso
Connoisseur	6	50	Toro
Torpedo	6¼	52	Figurado

Gourmet Lonsdale

PAUL GARMIRIAN (PG)
[CONTINUED]

1 Gourmet Belicoso Fino   **2** Gourmet 15th Anniversary Connoisseur
3 Gourmet Maduro Celebration Maduro

PUNCH [CUBA/HONDURAS]

P unch cigars were founded in 1840, and were named after the cantankerous yet popular puppet character Mr Punch. The brand was aimed specifically at the British market. Punch is the second-oldest Cuban brand (after Por Larranaga) and was bought in 1884 by Manuel López. López retired in 1924 and the brand

PUNCH (DELUXE)
Medium Honduras/Dominican Rep/Nicaragua
Connecticut Broadleaf Ecuador

Name	Length/Inches	Ring Gauge	Shape
Royal Coronation	5¼	44	Corona
Château M	5¾	45	Grand Corona
Château L	7¼	54	Double Corona

PUNCH (GRAND CRU)
Medium Honduras/Dominican Rep/Nicaragua
Connecticut Broadleaf Connecticut Shade

Name	Length/Inches	Ring Gauge	Shape
Punchito	4	50	Figurado
Robusto	5¼	50	Robusto
Superior	5⅝	47	Grand Corona
No. II	6⅛	54	Toro
Monarcas	6¾	48	Churchill
Prince Consort	8½	52	Giant

PUNCH (RARE COROJO)
Medium Honduras/Dominican Rep/Nicaragua
Connecticut Broadleaf Ecuador

Name	Length/Inches	Ring Gauge	Shape
Rothschild	4½	48	Robusto
Magnum	5¼	54	Robusto
El Doble	6	60	Super Robusto
Pita	6⅛	50	Toro
Double Corona	6¾	48	Double Corona

PUNCH (GRAN PURO)
Medium Honduras Honduras Honduras

Name	Length/Inches	Ring Gauge	Shape
Santa Rita	4½	52	Robusto
Rancho	5½	54	Robusto
Pico Bonito	6	50	Toro
Sierra	6½	48	Toro

Cuban Double Corona

was bought in 1930 by Fernández y Palicio, who also owned the successful Hoyo de Monterrey brand. Under their stewardship Punch cigars continued to sell well. Cuban Punch cigars are generally full and rich, and notable among the range is the Punch Double Corona, the Punch Punch and the Punch Churchill.

Honduran Punch cigars presently come in five series: the standard Punch, which uses an Ecuadorian Sumatra-seed wrapper, Honduran, Nicaraguan and Dominican filler, and Connecticut Broadleaf binder; the Punch Deluxe, similar to the standard but slightly fuller bodied and available in both natural and maduro wrappers; the smoother Grand Cru, also available in natural and maduro wrappers; the square-pressed and powerful Rare Corojo, which features extra rich and dark Ecuadorian wrappers; and the all-Honduran Gran Puro.

Cuban Petit Punch

PUNCH (CUBA)
📄 🌑 Medium ◉ Cuba 🌀 Cuba 🌑 Cuba

Name	Length/Inches	Ring Gauge	Shape
Petit Punch	4	40	Perla
Royal Selection No. 12	5	42	Mareva
Coronation	5	42	Mareva
Corona	5$\frac{1}{2}$	42	Corona
Royal Coronation	5$\frac{1}{2}$	42	Corona
Punch Punch	5$\frac{3}{5}$	46	Corona Gorda
Super Selection No. 1	6$\frac{1}{8}$	42	Corona Grande
Ninfas	7	33	Ninfa
Monarca	7	47	Julieta
Churchill	7	47	Julieta
Double Corona	7$\frac{3}{5}$	49	Prominente

PUNCH (HONDURAS)
📄 🌑 Medium ◉ Honduras/Dominican Rep/Nicaragua
🌀 Connecticut Broadleaf 🌑 Ecuador

Name	Length/Inches	Ring Gauge	Shape
Rothschild	4$\frac{1}{2}$	48	Robusto
Champion	4$\frac{1}{2}$	60	Figurado
London Club	5	40	Petit Corona
Magnum	5$\frac{1}{4}$	54	Robusto
Café Royale	5$\frac{5}{8}$	45	Grand Corona
Pita	6$\frac{1}{8}$	50	Toro
Punch	6$\frac{1}{4}$	45	Grand Corona
Lonsdale	6$\frac{1}{2}$	43	Lonsdale
Double Corona	6$\frac{3}{4}$	48	Double Corona
After Dinner	7$\frac{1}{4}$	46	Churchill
Presidente	8$\frac{1}{2}$	52	Giant

1 Cuban Punch Punch **2** Cuban Ninfas
3 Cuban Coronation (Tubo)

RAFAEL GONZALEZ [CUBA]

Lonsdale

The Rafael González brand started life in the late 1920s as La Flor de Marquez, but by 1945 had become Rafael González. The brand, like so many other Cuban brands, was created with one eye very firmly on the British market, and is notable for the long inscription on the box, part of which warns against a premium cigar's 'period of sickness'. It reads: 'These Cigars have been manufactured from a secret blend of pure Vuelta Abajo tobaccos selected by the Marquez Rafael González, Grandee of Spain. For more than 20 years this brand has existed. In order that the Connoisseur may fully appreciate the perfect fragrance they should be smoked either within one month of the date of shipment from Havana or should be carefully matured for about one year.' In actual fact it is doubtful that a real Marquez existed, the name being used as a marketing tool.

It is thought that the Rafael González brand is also responsible for creating the Lonsdale vitola (similar to the Cervantes), in honour of Hugh Cecil Lowther, the fifth Earl of Lonsdale, whose portrait used to appear on the box.

Romeo y Julieta

The cigars are manufactured in the Briones Montoto factory (formerly Romeo y Julieta), and have earned a deserved reputation for offering good value for money. Many aficionados compare the spicy, complex aroma of this cigar with that of a Montecristo; however, the latter is a much fuller-bodied cigar. Rafael González cigars are among the mildest Cuban cigars available and are ideal for someone new to Havanas.

RAFAEL GONZALEZ
📖 🍸 Mild to Medium ◉ Cuba 🌀 Cuba 🌑 Cuba

Name	Length/Inches	Ring Gauge	Shape
Très Petit Lonsdale	4½	40	Franciscano
Panatela Extra	5	37	Veguerito
Petit Corona	5	42	Mareva
Corona Extra	5⅝	46	Corona Gorda
Lonsdale	6½	42	Cervantes
Slenderella	7	28	Panatela Larga

RAMON ALLONES [CUBA/DOMINICAN REPUBLIC]

Despite dating back to around 1845, the Ramón Allones brand is relatively unknown outside connoisseurs' circles, but is a well-respected, mid-priced cigar all the same. The brand is notable for being the first to package its cigars in the now famous 8-9-8 configuration. The founder Ramón Allones is generally also accepted as being the first cigar producer to decorate his cedar wood boxes with a colourful painting.

Like Partagás cigars, the Ramón Allones line are produced in the Partagás factory. This fact may help explain why, like Partagás, these are among the fullest-bodied Havanas on the market. All of the Allones cigars are known for their distinctive flavour, but the Gigantes and the Specially Selected particularly favoured.

Dominican

In Cuba the brand was owned by Ramón Cifuentes, who sold the US rights to General Cigar Co. after he fled Cuba following the Revolution. The Dominican cigars use a Dominican wrapper grown specifically for the brand, a Connecticut Broadleaf binder, and ligero filler from Nicaragua and the Dominican Republic. The cigars are only available in larger gauges, and are a rich, full-bodied smoke.

Cuban Ramonitas

RAMON ALLONES (CUBAN)

📭 Ⓢ Full-bodied ◉ Cuba ◙ Cuba ◯ Cuba

Name	Length/Inches	Ring Gauge	Shape
Ramonitas	4³⁄₄	26	Carolina
Small Club Corona	4³⁄₈	42	Minuto
Allones Specially Selected	5	50	Robusto
Petit Corona	5	42	Mareva
Corona Extra	5³⁄₈	46	Corona Gorda
Belicosos	5¹⁄₂	52	Campana
Lonsdale	6³⁄₈	42	Cervantes
Gigantes	7³⁄₅	49	Double Corona

RAMON ALLONES (DOMINICAN)

📭 Ⓢ Mild to Medium ◉ Dominican Rep/Nicaragua
◙ Connecticut Broadleaf ◯ Dominican Rep

Name	Length/Inches	Ring Gauge	Shape
Gustoso	5	50	Robusto
Maestro	5¹⁄₂	54	Robusto
Brioso	6	45	Grand Corona
Ultimo	6¹⁄₂	49	Toro

RAMON ALLONES [CONTINUED]

1 Cuban Small Club Corona   **2** Cuban Allones Specially Selected
3 Cuban Belicosos   **4** Cuban Gigantes

ROMEO Y JULIETA [CUBA/DOMINICAN REPUBLIC]

Romeo y Julieta is one of the best known of all the Havana brands. Founded in 1875 (also making it one of the oldest), Romeo y Julieta presently makes 14 different types of hand-made vitolas (not including limited editions), putting the brand on a par with Partagás as one of the most prolific of premium cigars.

'Pepin' Rodríguez Fernandez

The brand's early success owes much to the dogged determination of José 'Pepin' Rodríguez Fernandez, who acquired the brand in 1903. Within two years he and his 1,400 employees were forced to move to a larger factory. Pepin travelled extensively throughout Europe in order to market his cigars, and as a special service for his wealthiest clients he would produce cigars with their own customized bands; indeed, at one stage he was manufacturing cigars with 2,000 different personalized bands. His frequently extravagant marketing tactics were exemplified by the fact that each year up until the start of World War II he would erect a stand under the balcony of the House of Capulet in Verona, a key setting for the Shakespeare play of the same name.

Cuba Cedros No. 3

ROMEO Y JULIETA (CUBA)
📄 🅢 Mild to Medium ◉ Cuba ◍ Cuba ◌ Cuba

Name	Length/Inches	Ring Gauge	Shape
Petit Julieta	4	30	Entreacto
Petit Princes	4	40	Perla
Très Petit Corona	4½	40	Franciscano
Short Churchill	4⁴/₅	50	Robusto
Cedros No. 3	5	42	Mareva
Petit Corona	5	42	Mareva
No. 2	5	42	Mareva
Exhibición No. 4	5	48	Hermoso No. 4
Petit Pirámide	5	50	Figurado
Corona	5½	42	Corona
Cedros No. 3	5½	42	Corona
Exhibición No. 3	5½	46	Corona Gorda
Belicoso	5½	52	Belicoso
Hermoso No. 2	6¼	48	Hermoso No. 2
Cazadore	6⁵/₈	44	Cazadore
Cedros No. 1	6½	42	Cervante
Hermoso No. 1	6⁵/₈	48	Hermoso No. 1
Churchill	7	47	Julieta

Cuban Churchill (Tubo)

Churchill

The brand continued to gain in popularity throughout much of the twentieth century, particularly in Britain, and its flagship Churchill cigar, widely regarded as the best cigar of that particular vitola, was named after one of the brand's most passionate and famous

ROMEO Y JULIETA (1875)
📄 🚬 Mild to Medium ⊙ Dominican Rep ◙ Dominican Rep
◖ Indonesia

Name	Length/Inches	Ring Gauge	Shape
Romeo	4	30	Small Panatela
Bully	5	50	Robusto
Romeo's Court	5½	44	Corona
Toro Exhibicion No. 3	6	50	Toro
Deluxe No. 2 (Glass tube)	6	50	Toro
Belicoso	6⅛	54	Belicoso
Lancero	6½	38	Panatela
Cedro deluxe No. 1	6½	44	Lonsdale
Churchill	7	50	Churchill
Exhibición No. 1	8½	52	Giant

ROMEO Y JULIETA (RESERVE MADURO)
📄 🚬 Mild to Medium ⊙ Dominican Rep/Nicaragua/Peru
◙ Nicaragua ◖ Connecticut Broadleaf

Name	Length/Inches	Ring Gauge	Shape
No. 4	5	44	Petit Corona
Petite Robusto	4¼	52	Robusto
Robusto	5	50	Robusto
Toro	6	50	Toro
Mini Belicoso	5	52	Belicoso
Belicoso	6⅛	52	Belicoso
Lonsdale	6⅝	44	Lonsdale
Churchill	7	50	Double Corona

ROMEO Y JULIETA (VINTAGE MADURO)
📄 🚬 Mild to Medium ⊙ Dominican Rep/Nicaragua/Peru
◙ Ecuador ◖ Connecticut Broadleaf

Name	Length/Inches	Ring Gauge	Shape
III	5	50	Robusto
I	6	43	Long Corona
II	6	46	Grand Corona
VII	6	50	Toro
VI	6½	60	Figurado
IV	7	48	Churchill
V	7½	50	Double Corona

ROMEO Y JULIETA (VINTAGE)
Mild to Medium ● Dominican Rep ● Mexico ○ Ecuador

Name	Length/Inches	Ring Gauge	Shape
III	5	50	Robusto
I	6	43	Long Corona
II	6	46	Grand Corona
VII	6	50	Toro
VI	6½	60	Figurado
IV	7	48	Churchill
V	7½	50	Double Corona

ROMEO Y JULIETA (ANIVERSARIO)
Mild to Medium ● Dominican Rep/Nicaragua/Peru
● Connecticut Broadleaf ○ Ecuador

Name	Length/Inches	Ring Gauge	Shape
Robusto	5	52	Robusto
Corona	5½	44	Corona
Toro	6	54	Toro
No. 2	6⅛	52	Belicoso
Churchill	7	54	Double Corona

ROMEO Y JULIETA (RESERVA REAL)
Mild to Medium ● Dominican Rep/Nicaragua ● Nicaragua
○ Ecuador

Name	Length/Inches	Ring Gauge	Shape
Lancero	4½	38	Lancero
Robusto	5	52	Robusto
Corona	5½	44	Corona
Toro	6	54	Toro
Lonsdale	6⅝	44	Lonsdale
Churchill	7	50	Double Corona

Cuban Belicoso

devotees, Sir Winston Churchill. Pepin died in 1954 at the age of 88, and following the Cuban Revolution the brand was brought under the ownership of Cubatabaco.

Today the cigar remains one of Cuba's best-selling brands, and in its honour a new vitola was created in 2006 – a robusto known as the Short Churchill. With such a wide variety of cigars, there's usually a 'Romeo' for just about every occasion, from the mild Cedros line to the full-bodied but deceptively smooth Churchills.

Dominican

The US rights to the brand are now owned by Altadis USA, and it is that company's biggest-selling hand-made brand. Dominican

Cuban Petite Julieta

'Romeos' come in a huge number of different shapes and sizes. There are at present six different Romeo y Julieta lines. The standard 1875 range is made with Dominican filler and binder, and an Indonesian TBN wrapper. The Reserve Maduros come in a blackened Connecticut Broadleaf wrapper, around a Nicaraguan binder, and a blend of Nicaraguan, Peruvian and Dominican filler. Similar are the wrappers of the Vintage Maduros, but they feature older filler and an Ecuadorian Sumatra-seed binder (and are available in a humidified cabinet). The Vintage range, featuring an Ecuadorian Connecticut Shade wrapper, Mexican binder and Dominican filler, are for the more experienced smoker. The recent Aniversario and Reserva Real also feature an Ecuadorian Connecticut Shade wrapper; the former uses a Connecticut Broadleaf binder and filler from the Dominican Republic, Peru and Nicaragua, and the latter, a binder from Nicaragua and filler from the Dominican Republic and Nicaragua. Another recent range, the Habana Reserve cigars, is almost pure Nicaraguan, featuring Nicaraguan wrappers, binder and filler, but with the filler also featuring some Honduran tobacco.

Edicion Limitada
Finally Altadis have announced a Limited Edition range of three vitolas, all tubed. They feature San Andres Corojo wrappers from Mexico, Connecticut Broadleaf binder, and filler from Nicaragua and the Dominican Republic.

ROMEO Y JULIETA (HABANA RESERVE)
📄 Ⓢ Medium to Full-bodied ◉ Honduras/Nicaragua
◉ Nicaragua ◯ Nicaragua

Name	Length/Inches	Ring Gauge	Shape
Robusto	5	54	Robusto
Corona	5⅝	45	Grand Corona
Toro	6	56	Toro
Belicoso	6⅛	52	Belicoso
Churchill	7	54	Double Corona

ROMEO Y JULIETA (EDICION LIMITADA)
📄 Ⓢ Mild to Medium ◉ Dominican Rep/Nicaragua
◉ Connecticut Broadleaf ◯ Mexico

Name	Length/Inches	Ring Gauge	Shape
Rothchilde (Tube)	5	54	Robusto
Prominente (Tube)	6	64	Toro
No. 2 (Tube)	5	52	Toro

1 Cuban Exhibición No. 3 2 Cuban Hermoso No. 2
3 Cuban No. 2 (Tubo) 4 Cuban Short Churchill

SAINT LUIS REY [CUBA/HONDURAS]

Another highly respected Cuban brand, Saint Luis Rey was founded in the mid-1950s by the British cigar importers Michael de Keyser and Nat Silverstone. The brand is relatively inexpensive compared with other Havanas, and has built up a following among cigar aficionados. Made at the Briones Montoto factory (formerly Romeo y Julieta), there are at present only six vitolas, all with a full-bodied yet smooth flavour. Churchill and Regio are generally considered the finest. Honduran Saint Luis Reys appeared in the late 1990s. After the 'crash' of 1999 the brand fell out of production, but has since been revived by Altadis USA who currently own the US rights. The cigars score consistently well for their price and are presently available in the standard Serie G lines.

Serie G Short Robusto

SAINT LUIS REY (CUBAN)
📄 Ⓢ Full-bodied ◉ Cuba ◍ Cuba ◖ Cuba

Name	Length/Inches	Ring Gauge	Shape
Petit Corona	5	42	Petit Corona
Regio	5	48	Robusto
Corona	5⅝	42	Corona
Serie A	5⅝	46	Corona Gorda
Lonsdale	6½	42	Cervante
Churchill	7	47	Julieta

SAINT LUIS REY (HONDURAN)
📄 Ⓢ Medium to Full-bodied ◉ Honduras/Nicaragua/Peru ◍ Nicaragua ◖ (Natural) Nicaragua (Maduro) Mexico

Name	Length/Inches	Ring Gauge	Shape
Rothchilde	5	54	Robusto
Corona	5¼	44	Corona
Titan	5½	60	Super Robusto
Toro	6	50	Toro
Belicoso	6⅛	52	Belicoso
Churchill	7	52	Double Corona

SAINT LUIS REY (SERIE G)
📄 Ⓢ Full-bodied ◉ Nicaragua ◍ Connecticut Broadleaf ◖ Connecticut Broadleaf

Name	Length/Inches	Ring Gauge	Shape
Short Robusto	4¼	54	Robusto
Rothchilde	5	56	Robusto
No. 6	6	60	Super Robusto
Belicoso	6⅛	54	Belicoso

SANCHO PANZA [CUBA/HONDURAS]

F ounded around 1850, the Sancho Panza brand is named after the faithful squire to Cervantes' mock-heroic figure Don Quixote, in the novel of the same name. Although one of Havana's oldest brands, it remains a relative unknown, not helped by the fact that the cigars are only available in a few countries.

Honduras

Unusually, the non-Cuban Sancho Panzas are much fuller bodied than their Cuban counterparts. Owned by Villazon & Co., part of General Cigar Co, Sancho Panzas have been developed under the experienced eye of Estelo Padrón and presently come in three varieties: the standard Sancho Panza, which features Honduran, Nicaraguan and Dominican filler, Connecticut Broadleaf binder and a Connecticut Shade wrapper; the Double Maduro, which also uses the Connecticut Broadleaf binder and a Connecticut Shade wrapper; and the recent Extra Fuerte, which is pure Honduran and the most robust of all the Honduran brands.

Cuba Non Plus

SANCHO PANZA (HONDURAN)
📄 🛇 Medium ◉ Honduras/Nicaragua/Dominican Rep
🍂 Connecticut Broadleaf 🛇 Connecticut Shade

Name	Length/Inches	Ring Gauge	Shape
Valiente	5¼	50	Robusto
Glorioso	6⅛	50	Toro
Caballero	6¼	45	Belicoso
Dulcinea	6¼	54	Corona
Primoroso	6⅜	47	Grand Corona

SANCHO PANZA (EXTRA FUERTE)
📄 🛇 Full-bodied ◉ Honduras 🍂 Honduras 🛇 Honduras

Name	Length/Inches	Ring Gauge	Shape
Valiente	5¼	50	Robusto
Glorioso	6⅛	50	Toro
Caballero	6¼	45	Belicoso
Dulcinea	6¼	54	Corona
Primoroso	6¾	47	Grand Corona

Honduran Caballero

A mild smoke

Although often thought of as too mild and lacking in flavour for the connoisseur, many appreciate the more subtle floral aromas of the Sancho Panza and it's an ideal Cuban cigar for a novice to start on. The brand is also notable for being one of the few to regularly produce a Belicoso Figurado and a Gran Corona, or giant vitola; the Sancho measures 9¼ inches.

SANCHO PANZA (DOUBLE MADURO)

📄 Ⓢ Medium ⦿ Honduras/Nicaragua/Dominican Rep
◐ Connecticut Shade ◒ Connecticut Broadleaf

Name	Length/Inches	Ring Gauge	Shape
Quixote	4½	50	Robusto
La Mancha	5½	44	Corona
Cervantes	6½	48	Toro
Escudero	7¼	54	Double Corona

SANCHO PANZA (CUBAN)

📄 Ⓢ Mild ⦿ Cuba ◑ Cuba ◒ Cuba

Name	Length/Inches	Ring Gauge	Shape
Non Plus	5⅛	42	Petit Corona
Corona	5⅝	42	Corona
Molino	6½	42	Cervante
Belicoso	5½	52	Belicoso
Corona Gigante	7	47	Julieta
Sancho	9¼	47	Gran Corona

1 Cuban Sancho **2** Cuban Corona Gigante **3** Cuban Belicoso **4** Cuban Corona

SAN CRISTOBAL DE LA HABANA [CUBA]

Oficios

The most recent Cuban cigar to be launched, following Cuaba (1996), Vegas Robaina (1997) and Trinidad (1998), San Cristóbal first appeared in 1999. The latest brand was targeted to fill the low-to-medium price point, Vegas Robaina and Trinidad having very much fitted into the higher end of the cigar market. And although the early cigars utilized tobacco from the Remedios region and were indeed very competitively priced, more recently the cigars have used tobacco from the more famous Vuelta Abajo region and consequently are now priced on a par with Bolívar and Sancho Panza.

Cuban landmarks

Named after Christopher Columbus and to mark the founding of Havana, initially the brand was launched with four vitolas – El Principe, La Fuerza, La Punta and El Morro – all named after famous Cuban castles that had at one time or another played a significant role in Cuba's history. The cigars were very well received – offering robust and powerful flavours. Two of the shapes were entirely new Cuban vitolas – La Fuerza can only be described as a long robusto, and El Morro, which has a double corona gauge and is longer than a julieta. Three more cigars have been added to the initial range, and following the trend for naming the cigars after famous Cuban landmarks, have been named after famous streets in Old Havana.

SAN CRISTOBAL DE LA HABANA
📄 Ⓢ Medium to Full-bodied ◉ Cuba ◕ Cuba ◯ Cuba

Name	Length/Inches	Ring Gauge	Shape
El Principe	4³⁄₈	42	Minuto
La Fuerza	5¹⁄₂	50	Robusto/Gordito
La Punta	5¹⁄₂	52	Campana
Oficios	5¹⁄₄	43	Oficios
Mercaderes	6¹⁄₂	48	Mercaderes
El Morro	7	49	Julieta
Murralla	7	54	Rodolf

1 El Morro **2** La Fuerza **3** La Punta **4** El Principe

SANTA DAMIANA [DOMINICAN REPUBLIC]

Panatela

Originally the brand name for a series of Cuban cigars, which no longer exists, Santa Damiana are now made exclusively in the Dominican Republic for Altadis USA. There are two series, the lighter, milder line, which is predominantly targeted at the American market, and the slightly more robust, fuller-bodied versions, which are aimed at Europe.

The frontmark for the American lines are numbered, such as Selección No. 100, No. 300 and so forth. They feature a Connecticut Shade wrapper and binder, and filler from the Dominican Republic.

Europe

Santa Damianas bound for Europe, particularly Britain, have more traditional names such as Robusto, Churchill and Corona, which although also utilizing a Connecticut Shade wrapper, have a slightly fuller-flavoured filler. All Santa Damianas have a reputation for good, consistent construction, the brand being rolled at the state-of-the-art Dominican La Romana factory.

SANTA DAMIANA

Mild to Medium ● Dominican Rep ● Dominican Rep ○ Connecticut Shade

Name	Length/Inches	Ring Gauge	Shape
Panatela	4½	36	Panatela
Petit Corona	5	42	Petit Corona
Robusto	5	50	Robusto
No. 500	5	50	Robusto
Corona	5⅛	42	Corona
No. 300	5½	46	Corona Extra
No. 600	6	50	Toro
No. 100	6¾	48	Toro
Torpedo	6⅛	52	Figurado
No. 700	6⅝	44	Lonsdale
Churchill	7	48	Churchill

SANTA DAMIANA (HABANA 2000)

Medium ● Dominican Rep/Brazil ● Nicaragua ○ Nicaragua

Name	Length/Inches	Ring Gauge	Shape
Rothschild	5¼	52	Robusto
Torbusto	5½	60	Super Robusto
Director	6¾	44	Lonsdale
Belicoso	7	52	Belicoso

1 Torpedo **2** Churchill **3** Corona **4** Robusto

TRINIDAD [CUBA/DOMINICAN REPUBLIC]

Maduro Toro

First exported in 1999, Trinidads were initially made at the El Laguito factory, home to Cohíba, moving to Pinar del Río in 2004. There was only one size, the Fundadore, a new vitola, slightly larger than the Cohíba Lancero. Three new sizes were added in 2003: the Reyes, Coloniales and Robusto Extra. Dominican Trinidads were first made in 1997 by Arturo Fuente. In 2003 Altadis USA bought the US rights to the brand, having taken over production in 2002. The medium-strength natural cigars feature Nicaraguan, Dominican and Peruvian filler, Connecticut Broadleaf binder and a Sumatran-shade Ecuador wrapper. The stronger maduros feature an Ecuadorian binder and a Connecticut Broadleaf wrapper.

TRINIDAD (CUBAN)
Medium to Full-bodied Cuba Cuba Cuba

Name	Length/Inches	Ring Gauge	Shape
Reyes	4³⁄₈	40	Rey
Coloniales	5¼	44	Mareva
Robusto Extra	6⅛	50	Super Robusto
Fundadores	7½	40	Laguito Especial

TRINIDAD (DOMINICAN)
Medium Nicaragua/Dominican Rep/Peru Connecticut Broadleaf Ecuador

Name	Length/Inches	Ring Gauge	Shape
Corona	5	44	Corona
Robusto	5	50	Robusto
Mini Belicoso	5	52	Belicoso
Toro	6	50	Toro
Belicoso	6⅛	52	Belicoso
Lonsdale	6⅝	44	Lonsdale
Churchill	7	50	Double Corona
Fundadores	7½	40	Giant Corona

TRINIDAD (MADURO)
Medium Nicaragua/Dominican Rep/Peru Ecuador Connecticut Broadleaf

Name	Length/Inches	Ring Gauge	Shape
Trini Petite	4	30	Small Panatela
Petite Robusto	4¼	54	Robusto
Toro	6	55	Toro
Belicoso	6⅛	54	Belicoso
Churchill	7	58	Double Corona

1 Cuba Fundadores **2** Cuba Robusto Extra
3 Cuba Coloniales **4** Cuba Reyes

VEGAS ROBAINA [CUBA]

Named in honour of Cuba's most famous tobacco farmer, Alejandro Robaina, the Vegas Robaina brand was first launched in 1997 with the Spanish market in mind. The box features a portrait of Robaina, who for over 50 years has produced some of the finest wrapper leaves on his farm in Cuba's famous tobacco-growing region of Vuelta Abajo.

Generations

The land, situated near the town of San Luis, has been in the Robaina family since the middle of the nineteenth century, and has been passed down from father to son ever since. Alejandro himself inherited the land from his father Maruto in 1950, following his death, and has continued the work of producing among the most sought-after tobacco in the world.

The five vitolas (all hand-made) score consistently well in tastings around the world, with the Unico (a pyramid) performing particularly well. Full-bodied and rich, Vegas Robainas are said to use some of the best tobacco on the island, including wrappers from Robaina's own farm.

VEGAS ROBAINA
📄 💲 Medium to Full-bodied ◉ Cuba ◙ Cuba ◯ Cuba

Name	Length/Inches	Ring Gauge	Shape
Familiar	5⅝	42	Corona
Famoso	5	48	Hermoso No. 4
Unico	6⅛	52	Figurado
Clásico	6½	42	Cervante
Don Alejandro	7⅝	49	Prominente

Familiar

1 Don Alejandro **2** Clásico
3 Unico **4** Famoso

GLOSSARY

ACCORDION FOLD Name given to the way in which the filler leaves in a hand-rolled cigar are folded to ensure the cigar burns evenly and draws well.

BAND A decorative strip of paper wrapped near the head of the cigar. Bands are printed with the name of the brand and often help to indicate the cigar's country of origin. Smoking a cigar with the band on was once unfashionable, but now bands are usually left on to avoid the risk of damaging the wrapper.

BINDER One of the three types of tobacco used in a premium cigar. The binder leaves hold the bunch together.

BUNCH The collection of filler and binder leaves that form the main body of the cigar before the wrapper and cap are added.

BURROS Large square piles of fermenting tobacco up to 2 metres (7 feet) high. The temperature of the burros is carefully monitored; if the temperature reaches over 35°C (110°F) the pile is broken up to allow some of the excess heat to escape.

CABINET Type of cigar box.

CANDELA The name given to a pale green wrapper. The colour comes from the green chlorophyll in the wrapper leaf, which is biochemically fixed before the fermentation process. Also known as double *claro*.

CAP Made out of an unused piece of wrapper leaf, the cap stops the wrapper from unfurling. The cap must be cut to enable the cigar to draw.

CHAVETA A curved blade used by cigar rollers primarily to cut wrapper leaves.

CLARO A specific colour of wrapper leaf. *Claro* wrappers are usually grown in the shade and are light brown in colour. They are often referred to as 'natural' wrappers.

COLORADO A specific colour of wrapper leaf. *Colorado* wrappers are medium reddish-brown in colour and are usually used on well-matured cigars.

COLORADO CLARO A specific colour of wrapper leaf. *Colorado claro* wrappers are lighter than colorado but darker than *claro* wrappers.

CONNECTICUT BROADLEAF A type of wrapper leaf grown only in the Connecticut River valley region in the United States. Unlike Connecticut Shade, which is darker in colour, Connecticut Broadleaf is fully exposed to the sun as it grows. It is often used to wrap *maduro* cigars.

CONNECTICUT SHADE A type of wrapper leaf grown only in the Connecticut River valley region in the United States. It is so-called because it is grown under muslin-like material. Connecticut Shade wrapper leaves are light in colour and are used in mild- to medium-strength cigars. Connecticut Shade is among the most expensive tobacco in the world.

COROJO A variety of tobacco plant.

CRIOLLO A variety of tobacco plant.

CUBAN SEED Tobacco plants grown anywhere in the world other than Cuba, but using seeds originating from Cuba.

CULEBRAS Rare form of cigar, which actually comprises of three cigars woven together.

DOUBLE CLARO *See* candela.

DRAW Term used to describe the airflow through a cigar. A good hand-rolled cigar should draw easily, yet not so easily that the smoke is hot.

ESCAPARTE A room or cabinet where cigars condition for a few weeks after being rolled in order to expel any moisture that the tobacco may have picked up in the factory.

FERMENTATION Biochemical process, similar to composting. Most tobacco will undergo two periods of fermentation, during which ammonia in the tobacco is released and the amount of nicotine falls.

FIGURADO Term used to describe any irregular-shaped cigar. The most common *figurados* are pyramids (*pirámides*), *perfectos* and *culebras*.

FILLER Tobacco leaf, which together with the binder, forms a cigar's bunch. Filler leaves in hand-rolled cigars are long and uncut and are folded in a certain way to allow the cigar to draw evenly. The filler leaf gives the cigar most of its flavour.

FOOT The end of the cigar that is lit.

HEAD The capped end of the cigar.

HUMIDOR A cabinet or room in which the humidity and temperature are carefully maintained. Opinion varies slightly on the correct levels, but a humidity of 70 per cent and temperature of between 20°C/66°F and 21°/70°F will keep cigars from drying out.

LECTOR This literally means 'reader' and refers to a person who reads aloud to the cigar rollers. Beginning in the mid-nineteenth century in Havana, lectors would read a variety of material ranging from novels to newspapers. During the Cuban Revolution lectors were largely to thank for keeping cigar factory workers informed. The practice is not as widespread as it once was.

LIGERO The top leaves of a tobacco plant. *Ligero* tobacco is stronger and has more flavour than leaves from lower down the plant.

MADURO A specific shade of wrapper leaf. *Maduro* wrappers are dark, reddish brown.

OSCURO A specific shade of wrapper leaf. *Oscuro* wrappers are almost black.

PAREJOS A straight-sided cigar as opposed to a shaped cigar or *figurado*.

PERFECTO A figurado cigar that is closed at both ends, and which usually bulges in the middle.

PYRAMID (PIRAMIDE) A *figurado* cigar that is wider at the foot than it is at the head.

PLUG A knot of tobacco in a cigar that stops it drawing properly. Plugs can be felt if the cigar is rolled gently between the fingers, and can sometimes be cleared by gently rolling the cigar.

RING GAUGE The diameter of a cigar measured in $1/64$ ths of an inch; hence a cigar with a ring gauge of 32 is $1/2$-inch wide.

TERCIOS Large square bales of fermented tobacco, wrapped in palm bark to keep the tobacco at a constant humidity. Tobacco is sent to factories in the form of *tercios*.

TORCEDORE(A) A cigar roller.

TUBOS Cigars packaged in aluminium tubes. They are also often wrapped in a very thin layer of cedar.

WRAPPER The tobacco leaf that is placed around the filler and binder. Wrapper leaves are often the most expensive tobacco in a cigar because of the many selection processes it goes through.

INDEX

ACKNOWLEDGEMENTS

The publisher would like to thank the following for permission to reproduce copyright material: Alamy: John Birdsall 56; Kathleen Watmough/Aliki image library 61; John James 65t; Images&Stories 67c; Martin Bobrovsky/INSADCO Photography 80. Corbis: Peter M. Wilson 2; Susana Vera/Reuters 4, 5; Fulvio Roiter 10; Alison Wright 11b; Theodor de Bry 11t; Historical Picture Archive 15; Brooklyn Museum 16; Bettmann 17b, 17t, 18b; The Art Archive 18; Phillip Spruyt Stapleton Collection 19t; Bettmann 20, 21b; Corbis 21t; Hulton-Deutsch Collection 22; Bettmann 23; Historical Picture Archive 24; Hans Georg Roth 25; Bettmann 25b, 26; Corbis 26t; Bettmann 27; Hulton-Deutsch Collection 27t; Art Photogravures Co. 28, 29; Richard Cummins 29b; Kevin Fleming 29t; Frances Benjamin Johnston 30; Patrick Robert/Sygma 31t; Dmitri Baltermants/The Dmitri Baltermants Collection 32; Bettmann 33b, 33t; Catherine Karnow 36; Charles & Josette Lenars 38, 39; Marion Post Wolcott 41t; E.O. Hoppé 42; Dave G. Houser 43; José F. Poblete 44b; Jan Butchofsky-Houser 44t; James Davis/Eye Ubiquitous 46; Reuters 47t; Najlah Feanny 48; Ronald Siemoneit 48b; Wally McNamee 49t; Jeremy Horner 50; Susana Vera/Reuters 51b; Christophe Boisvieux 51t; Rufus F. Folkks 52; Bettmann 53t; Hulton-Deutsch Collection 53b; Owen Franken 54, 55; Alejandro Ernesto/epa 57; Richard Hamilton Smith 58, 59; Kevin Fleming 59; James Sparshatt 60; Jeremy Horner 62; Patrick Robert/Sygma 63b, 64; JP Laffont/Sygma 63c, 65b, 66c; Dave G. Houser 66b; Claudia Daut/Reuters 67b, 67t; Bob Krist 68; Richard Bickel 69b; Owen Franken 70; Colin Garratt/ Milepost 92 ½ 71b; Patrick Robert/Sygma 72, 73t; Arne Hodalic 73b; Michael S. Yamashita 77t; Claudia Daut/Reuters 79t; Leif Skoogfors 81b, 81t; Macduff Everton 82; Michael S. Yamashita 83; Yves Gellie 84; Rafael Perez/Reuters 85t. Getty: Theodore de Bry/The Bridgeman Art Library 12; Alonso Sanchez Coello/The Bridgeman Art Library 13t; John Decritz the Elder/The Bridgeman Art Library 13b; English School/The Bridgeman Art Library 14; Don Hebert 8, 9; Dmitri Kessel/Time & Life Pictures 40; Bruno Morandi 86, 87; PicturePress 7t. Istock: 22, 46; John Rodriguez 76; W. Brian Watkins 88. Paul Miller: 66t, 69t, 71t. Rex Features: Louisa Macdonell 85b.

Grateful thanks to the following for supplying cigars and cigar images: Altadis USA/Don Diego; British American Tobacco/Dunhill; Davidoff of London; Arturo Fuente/Montesino; Felipe Gregorio; Gawith Hoggarth Tobacco Trading Ltd/Nat Sherman; Hunters & Frankau/Fonseca; Tor Imports/Sant Luis Rey; www.topcubans.com/ La Gloria Cubana.